PRINCIPAL WITH PRINCIPLES

AS IS THE PRINCIPAL SO IS THE INSTITUTE

RAJENDRA PRASAD DOBHAL

This book is dedicated to my GURUS, particularly the Principals under whose dynamic leadership I groomed and developed myself.

They have always been a source of inspiration for me. I am grateful for their valuable guidance, timely motivation and help. I have always been their true disciple and follower of their footprints.

Contents

Foreword

It gives me immense pleasure to place on record the commendable job done by Mr. R.P Dobhal in bringing out a perfect souvenir titled as 'Principal with Principles'. In fact the book is the compilation of his vast and varied experiences as a Teacher, Educational Administrator and Trainer. This is based on his own innovations and experimentations undertaken from time to time in various schools that he headed and training programs he conducted.

The book consists of the Principles, Ideals, Beliefs and Ethics that a principal must possess to become an effective person, professional, administrator, manager and leader. The principal is the person responsible for making great strides in the institution. He/She is the Institution Builder who conceptualizes and implements the ambitious plans for the growth and development of the Institution. Various Roles and Responsibilities of the Principal have been described in a very practical manner.

The book highlights several Managerial, Interpersonal and Leadership skills of Principal which assist him in enhancing Personal and Professional Effectiveness. In every chapter the emphasis has been laid on the Principal's commitments and competence to accomplish the Mission and Vision of the Institution.

I am sure the book provides very relevant and practical inputs to the principals to become excellent academicians, a good administrators and effective leaders.

If read between the lines, the principals, would be principals and aspiring principals will certainly be benefitted.

Mr. R.P Dobhal has also authored a book titled as "A Guide to Effective Teaching" consisting of the effective teaching learning strategies. The main focus in the book is on ' HOW TO TEACH' .

I wish him every success in his endeavour.

Shri Mahant Devendra Dass
Chancellor Shri Guru Ram Rai University,
&
Manager, SGRR Education Mission
Dehradun, Uttarakhand

Preface

As is the Principal, so is the School. The personality of a Principal reflects in the Institution he/she heads. The achievements of the school both in scholastic and co-scholastic spheres depend on the managerial and leadership skills of the Principal.

Quality Education is now a global phenomenon. Education is perhaps the most important indicator of economic, social and political development of a nation. An educated population not only contributes significantly to the growth and development of the nation but also adds to the effectiveness, efficiency and competence of the people.

Educational Institutions both academic and professional lay the foundation of overall development through the quality education imparted by them. Quality Education is impossible without quality teachers and quality Principals. The Institutions can realize the objectives of Quality Education when the planning and monitoring systems are not only effective but a very strong mechanisms have to be developed for the accomplishment of desired results. All this is possible when the person at the helm is a visionary and missionary. He/She has a vision to fulfill and a mission to achieve; therefore a Principal must have core beliefs, ideals, and principles which will help in making the Institution a learning organization.

In this book efforts have been made to incorporate all those principles, abilities and qualities which the Principal must possess to administer, monitor, supervise and guide.

CHAPTER I

Principal, The Key Person in the School

Who is the Principal ?

The Principal is the officer in-charge of all affairs of the Institution. He/She is not only responsible but also accountable for all round development i.e Academic Standard, Good Discipline, Execution of Policies, Rules ,Regulations and above all, the Cordial and Congenial Environment of the Institution.

Principal is the Head of the Institution and Expected to be 'The Head with Head'. A head smart person i.e is to have thorough knowledge of School Administration, Academic planning and Monitoring, Management Practices, Processes, Procedures and Policies.

Principal is the Chief Executive Officer (CEO) or the Chief Operating Officer (COO) of the institution. Both these terms are not only relevant to the Corporate Sector but also to an Academic Institution.

In Administrative Hierarchy the principal is the first holding the top position and highest rank in the school/college. He manages all affairs, gives directions, makes decisions and takes actions.

Principal is the controlling authority. All affairs of the institution are under the direct control of the principal. He exercises the powers assigned to control and administer. Therefore the Principal is the chief controller of all resources of the Institution.

Principal is the 'Father Figure' in the Institution. He/She is the 'Foster Parent' of students and staff, a Guardian and a Guide. He is the person who builds healthy relations and develops **belongingness.**

Principal is therefore -

- **An Academician**
- **An Administrator**

- **A Manager**
- **A Leader**
- **Above all - A Human Being**

Principal is the Wall Mirror for the staff and students. Principal guides, motivates, decides, delegates and therefore, the most responsible person in the Institution. Good Principal is always goal oriented rather than rule oriented.

All stakeholders very closely observe the walk, talk, behaviour action and accent of the Principal. Therefore, one has to be very particular and vigilant in this regard. Principal is an Institution in himself/herself.

The Dress and Address of the Principal is of paramount importance. The teachers and students are much impressed by this attribute. The approach of the Principal should be people centric for regeneration and rejuvenation. Thus the Principal is expected to be a remarkable person with overwhelming humility.

Principal must on all occasions display maturity and patience. The consistent and persistent efforts of the Principal not only contribute to the personal growth but the growth of the Institution as well.

Appear as you are, be as you appear. All our dreams come true if we have the courage to pursue them.

Understanding self, Self Respect, High Self Esteem are the core responsibilities of Principal to self. If you are not respectful towards yourself, your dreams and values, do not expect others to be respectful to you.

The Principal in the Institution is both an Observer and a Supervisor. As an Observer Principal has to keep an eye on each and every affair of the Institution. Keen observation of the Principal is essential for the progress of the Institution. As a Supervisor, the Principal has to supervise the quality of instructions, discipline and overall functioning.

Principal is an Educational Leader. He should be able to create a Dynamic School System by nurturing and sustaining the

processes of dialogue, decision making, action taking and evaluation that leads to overall improvement. The Educational Leadership is said to have succeeded in its endeavour if a sea change is business in the educational scenario in general and Quality Education in particular. This substantive change is team effort. Invaluable Trust and bestowing Confidence in team is of great importante. Therefore, the Principal must be aiming at achieving new heights of progressive and inclusive Institutional Development.

Principal should be looking out from within in order to inspire, motivate, guide and support. Must be connecting with self and others. He is expected to be high on both confidence and performance to make tangible contributions.

The Principal's role in providing access to Quality Education to students through Quality Teaching is of great significance. Effective Principal enables them to perform better to the best and excel in Teaching and Learning. For this purpose the Principal needs to broaden the areas of both scholastic and co scholastic spheres. Optimistic mood and healthy outlook are always helpful in overcoming numerous problems of the system. **Such an approach plays a pivotal role in setting the Bench Marks and reaching new Milestones.**

Rolling out ambitious schemes and chalking down the strategies for their effective implementation will foster Institutional Development, enhance professional growth and ultimately lead to Excellence in Education.

One who functions with an open heart and open mind, lets ego go away, loves, cares and lives in the present is a successful Principal. Giving sufficient impetus to the Process of Holistic Development is the **prerogative as well as the responsibility of the Principal.**

The importance of Principal in the Institution is just like the Back Bone in the body. Any defect in the back bone adversely affects the functioning of humans. Similarly the Institution suffers due to incompetence and ineffectiveness of the Principal.

It is suggested that the **Principal should follow the F A C T approach to** succeed ie:

Fact: Always put the facts first before the staff and students. Make them aware about the factual position of the problem/ situation that rises in the system.

Act: After having put the fact forward, the Principal has to work effectively for finding a suitable solution.

Contact: To communicate to the concerned about the decision made and action taken.

Tact: The Principal has to deal tactfully with the faculty and students so that the work is done and the problem is solved. **Tactful dealing is also a skill. It leads to Win Win Situation.**

Principal is the Captain of the Ship. Sailing or sinking of the ship by and large depends on the effectiveness or ineffectiveness of the Captain. With his vision, mission and capabilities the Principal can take the Institution to the stupendous level of success.

Now gone are the days of Bossism. The Principal is not the boss but the Leader of the Institution. One who is able to turn aspirations into Achievemcents always succeeds. Good Principals are able to handle the job with aplomb and are capable enough to come back after a set back.

Principal is a tall leader and Institution builder. A man of Integrity and excellent manners. Makes conscientious efforts to instil Trust in all stakeholders. The Institutions now need coaches not the bosses.

Principal is the Torch Bearer. Leads the way to success. Must have a strong sense of purpose and Commitment. Erratic behaviour and mood swings are harmful for self and others. The mettle of the Principal is tested everywhere and every time. An astute leader should reflect on the personality of the Principal. **Smart Working is expected in place of Hard Working.**

CHAPTER II

Roles and Responsibilities of Principal – Principal as an Academician

Role and Responsibility are two sides of the same coin. Both go together and are closely related to each other. Role is played ,Responsibility is Delivered.

In this era of cut-throat competition, every person at the helm has to play multi-dimensional roles in the system he/she heads. Similarly, the roles of principal are also varied. As described earlier, the roles of principal can be summed up as Academician, Administrator, Manager, Leader and A Person.

With every role, a number of responsibilities are attached. A competent and effective principal actively plays all the roles, understands the responsibilities and discharges them effectively.

Principal as an Academician - Academic Skills.

An Investment in Knowledge pays the Best Interest.

Benjamin Franklin

Principal is supposed to be the most knowledgeable person in the Institution. The Academic and Professional qualifications, Experience and Expertise of the Principal make him an Educationist.

The Principal is basically an academician, an academic leader. Renowned Principals are known for their academic accumenship and flair. The teacher in the Principal must not die. It has been noticed that many Principals give up teaching after assuming the office. This is very unfortunate on their part as well as on the part of students and teachers.

The Principal can guide and advise only when he himself is teaching and is aware of the innovative and interactive teaching and learning practices. The Principal must be a master of his/her subject. It would be appreciated if the Principal regularly teaches some periods of his own subject. It will not only set the tone but also set an example for the faculties.

Besides, the Principal must possess some basic knowledge of all other subjects being taught in the Institution. If the Principal is seriously interested, he or she will have a basic understanding of all these issues. This will facilitate the Principal in proper monitoring and supervision of academic activities.The Principal will be able to discharge his academic duties and responsibilities only when he possess the following skills :

Academic Planning Skills.

This is the first and foremost responsibility of the principal. Planning is a skill, the ability to do/perform.Academic planning includes -

· **Strategies for providing quality education and achieving academic excellence.**

· **Strengthening the support system and the facilities i.e labs, libraries, audio/video aids, ICT etc.**

· **Planning for textbooks and reference material**

· **Planning for co-curricular activities·**

. **Time-Table planning.**

· **Planning for coverage of syllabus and judicious revision.**

· **Testing/Exams and Evaluation·**

. **Creation of academic climate.**

Planning is said to be successful when it is implemented effectively. It has been often noticed that the planning is good but owing to ineffective implementation desired results are not achieved. Some of the features of good planning are:

It should be a continuous process.

It must be creative and flexible.

It is time bound.

It must be motivating.

People are the essence of planning.

Teaching Skills.

The Principal himself is a Head Teacher. He must be the best teacher in the school. Teaching should be his passion. The

Principal must not cease teaching. The Principal has to ascertain that the teaching practices of the teachers are effective, innovative and learner-centred.

Some of the teaching skills are listed below -

· **Presentation Skills... Principal is** expected to be a keen observer of the entire functioning in general and transactional work in particular, failing which the desired results become difficult to achieve.

· **Narration Skills... Principal's** narration should be clear and understandable. Whatever the Principal tells, verbally as well as in writing must convey a sense and meaning.

· **Drafting Skills..** Being head of the institution the Principal has to draft or get letters, circulars, orders, notes etc drafted . All these must display excellent drafting skills of the Principal.

· **Guiding Skills..**

Principal is not only a supervisor or observer but also a guide to the staff and students. Principal's guidance is most valuable because of his experience, expertise and exposure.

. **Observation Skills.**

Principal is expected to be a keen observer of the entire functioning in general and transactional work in particular. Failing which the desired results become difficult to achieve.. An effective principal simply takes rounds in classes and ensures the smooth conduct of teaching and learning practices on the basis of observations. The Principal can observe classroom transactions by seeing and listening to the students and teachers.

There is a substantial potential in everyone.If stimulating and exciting opportunities to grow and excel are provided, both the teachers and students can bring laurels in every sphere.

Principal must be able to design the Academic Planner meticulously so that the objectives of Quality Education and Academic Excellence become easy to achieve. Principal should be pitching for more and more reforms in all pedagogical concerns. Principal's Leadership qualities, academic flair and Administrative capabilities will certainly contribute significantly towards the overall growth of the Institution.

Principal is supposed to be the most knowledgeable person in the Institution. Besides, the Skills and Attitude of the Head are more important. These attributes motivate the teachers and students to seek guidance from time to time.

Supervision Skills.

The Principal is the supervisor of the school. Effective supervision will lead to quality education and academic excellence. The Principal's time management, interpersonal skills, and leadership skills will assist him/her to supervise the transactional work as well as the smooth functioning of the school efficiently.

Inspection Skills.

Inspecting the transactional work from time to time is one of the important responsibilities of the Principal. The Principal must inspect the classes and record the observations. An inspection can be a surprise, planned and informed.

Inspection tools and techniques adopted in this process must be planned and systematic. The observations recorded during the inspection must be brought to the notice of the concerned teachers so that they can improve and become effective.

Principal should be discharging duties with the firm conviction that Education is always instrumental to development of curiosity, instilling joy for learning and promoting sound character. Core values of Discipline, Integrity and holistic learning can be promoted through education.

Principal as an Academician must follow the Introspective and Accountable approach for raising the academic standard and setting the bench marks. He has to be logical and methodical. This will lighten the load of the Principal and develop a sense of responsibility in faculty. Principal must never ever limit his imagination. *Always expect more from self and less from others.*

CHAPTER III

Principal as a Manager

Principal manages all the affairs of the Institution he heads. Performs all managerial functions.

Who is a Manager?

Manager is one who handles the affairs of an Organization effectively and efficiently. He/she is responsible for the smooth functioning of the organisation.

Manager is one who gets the work done by others(team).

Manager is one who performs all Management Functions of Planning, Organising, Directing, Controlling and Evaluating.

Manager manages men, money and material.

In view of the above, Principal is a Manager because all above mentioned functions are performed by the Principal. Success of the Institution depends on the managerial competencies of the Principal.

Good managers not only perform but also transform and thus prove to be an asset to the Organization failing which inefficient managers can also become biggest liability.

Principal is the Top level Manager who coordinates with other stake holders for the smooth functioning. Therefore, Principal is both a manager and a leader.

Management is a multidimensional affair. There are various areas which the Principal has to manage. Principal is the Academic Manager, Personnel Manager, Finance Manager, Strategic Manager and many others.

Management is needed in every sphere of life. It is very essential for...

Proper utilization of resources.

Enhancing Performance and achieving goals.

Facing competition.

Quality assurance.

Initiating Research and Development.

Problem Solving.

Management is a skill and a complete Manager is one who possesses all managerial skills ie Conceptual, Technical, HR and Decision Making skills.

Academic Management..

This is the foremost sphere of management for the Principal. Principal has to ensure the quality of education being imparted, teaching learning strategies are effective and innovative, academic excellence is being achieved and the Institution is a learning Organization. All these are to be managed simultaneously.

Managing Academic Affairs is the foremost responsibility of the Principal as the name and fame of an educational Institution is directly related to its academic accomplishments. Both scholastic and coscholastic areas need to be managed in such an effective way that the results are excellent. Educational Institution is basically result oriented. Therefore, academic management is on the top of all other managerial affairs of the Institution.

A joke is often related to the standard of an Institution,

Once parents visited a Professional Institution in connection with the admission of their ward. Before consulting the concerned authority they wanted to gather feedback about the standard of the college. They met some other parents, faculty members and the visitors in the campus. But they were not much convinced. In the meanwhile someone suggested them to ask the gate keeper about the college as he is the oldest serving employee and knows everything about the college. With hesitation they went to him to gather some information. The gate keeper apprised them of the details of the college ie the standard, faculty, culture, facilities and all others. The parents came to know whatever they wanted. They asked him, "How do you know so much about this college"? 'I am an ex student of this college'. replied the gate keeper.

HRD Management..

Managing the Human Resources is another important management area. The success of an Institution by and large depends on managing Human Resources efficiently and effectively.

Every organization is people centric. People play key role in its functioning. HR management is to recruit the work force, their selection, placement, pay, perks, promotions, transfers, training, research and development etc. This is rather a very challenging field of management.

Principal being Head of the Institution, has to manage all these affairs directly or indirectly.

Financial Management

Principal is also the Manager Finance of the Institution. It is rather a difficult Branch of management. **Some people may take it as Dealing with Gold Mine buy it may also turned into working in Coal Mine.**

Financial Management consists of Procurement, Purchases, Budgeting, Accounting, Auditing etc. One has to be very careful while dealing with each of the these aspects. Principal is the chief financial controller.

Office Management

Office is to be managed in such a way that there is perfect coordination between the Principal and the office. Any misunderstanding and mis communication will adversely affect the functioning of the Institution.

Noting, drafting, reporting, recording, public relations are some of the important areas of Office Management. Principal has to ensure timely completion of work, office discipline and proper maintenance of records.

Strategic Management.

Strategy is a ploy of future course of action for survival and growth. It is developing a plan of action to decide the future of the Institution. While formulating strategy for development both explicit and implicit factors need to be taken into consideration. SWOT analysis of the organization is also essential.

Principal is also Strategic Manager. Strategic management is to plan and monitor the strategies for over all growth and development of the Institution. Targets/goals are to be set, strategies to accomplish the targets are to be planned, feed back mechanism is to be developed.Excellence in Education is the most important objective of any Educational Institution. Providing Quality Education is instrumental to this. Accomplishment if all this will directly depend on the strategies planned, implemented and monitored by the Principal.

Performance Management.

Principal being Head of the Institution is also responsible for the performance of the team headed. The assigned duties are done with full justification or not, desired results are achieved or not, work is being done timely with accuracy, remedies for poor performance, performance appraisal etc are the parts of Performance Management. Principal has to oversee each and every aspect of employees performance.

There are many other areas of Institutional Management which the Principal has to manage efficiently and effectively.

Technology Management.

Technology is the buzz word these days. All employees are expected to be technology savvy. Principal must also possess knowledge of technology. The employees need to update themselves in technological skills from time to time. Principal has to manage necessary tools, techniques and equipments for this. Technology plays a vital role in overall functioning of the Institution. It is now an instrument to solve a variety of problems. Digitization is an emergent need of the time. **Both Technology and Talent can take the organization to the highest level.**

Performance Management

Performance is the backbone of any Institution. In management it is often said, **'Perform or Perish'.** Valid and reliable measures are to be adopted to assess the Performance. Tackling poor and under performance, developing a mechanism, performance appraisal are some of the important aspects of Performance Management.

The role of Principal as a Manager is therefore, vast and varied. The managerial skills and professional capabilities of Principal certainly enable him/her to manage this vast sphere of Institutional Management.

Principal is expected to be the greatest Performer in the System. The achievements and accomplishments of an Institution depend on the overall performance of the Principal and the team. At the same time Principal is the reformer also. Reforms in the form of changes are introduced by the Principal.

Further a good and effective principal is one who:

Performs and reforms not by compulsion but by conviction.

Strengthens his /her Personal network.

Provides nurturing support, social and psychological security to the staff and students.

Builds pleasant work environment.

Establishes stronger bond with the stakeholders.

Functions without fear, favour and ill will.

Develops intelligence as well as diligence.

Finally

Do no wrong to anyone and don't let any wrong happen to you and the Institution.

CHAPTER IV

Principal as An Administrator

Administration is conducting, handling and controlling the affairs of the Institution.It is mainly concerned with the development of strategies, formulation of policies and their execution to achieve objectives.

Principal excutes the prescribed codal procedures and processes, administers the Institution with the help of given rules and regulations. Principal is the administrative head, takes all decisions, coordinates with all stake holders for smooth functioning. Principal has the authority to administer, direct and control all affairs of the Institution.

Decision making and action taking are two important administrative functions of the Principal. Being a controlling authority all major and minor decisions and actions are initiated by the Principal. The administrative responsibilities of the Principal can be summed up as under..

Formulating

This is the process of Ppanning and preparation for the identification of strategies to accomplish the long term as well as short term objectives of the Institution. The Principal formulates his own practices, ideas and opinions with in the prescribed framework to realize desired objectives.

Executing/Implementing

Principal is the front runner in implementing the reforms planned.The approach should be innovative and multidisciplinary. Principal executes the rules and regulations. He is the implementor of the planned strategies and exercises the authority in accordance to the rules.

Decision Making

This is the most important administrative responsibility of the Principal. Being an administrative head all major and minor decisions are taken by the Principal for the smooth functioning of the Institution. In fact the growth and development of the Institution is directly related to the wise and justified decisions of the Principal.

Stephen Covey has very rightly said ," I am not a product of my circumstances, I am the Product of my Decisions."

Hasty decisions are never fair. Haste makes waste. Don't judge anything by outward appreance. Principal should become more nimble in decision making.

A number of decisions are required to be taken by the Principal in day to day life. Some of them are pertaining to...

Disciplinary Decisions

Indiscipline is perhaps the major cause for an adverse functioning of any Institution. It can be both in students and staff. The Principal has to mend their ways in a befitting manner. The best possible strategies would be ....

Proper understanding of The problem.

Have a proper Dialogue with them.

Patient listening.

Allowing them to put forward their view points.

Not to be bias, be impartial.

Act Proactive rather than Reactive.

Stringent Actions must be taken against dereliction of duties. In fact all this will depend on the Potentials and Initiatives of the Principal.

Academic Decisions

Principal is the key person to take decisions about the strategies for realizing the Academic Objectives of the Institution. An Institution earns reputation, name and fame mainly due to its academic achievements. Principal being Academic Leader has to take decisions about..

Achieving Academic Excellence

Providing Quality Education.

Effective Teaching Learning Strategies.

Faculty Development Programs.

Administrative Decisions..

Principal is also the Administrative Head.The decisions pertaining to the effective implementation or rules, regulations, codal formalities etc are taken by the Principal.

Financial Decisions

Principal is the Finance Manager. He/she has to ascertain proper utilization of allotted funds, Head wise distribution, budgeting, accounting and auditing.

Strategic Decisions

The Principal has to set long term as well as short term goals and strategies to accomplish them. It also includes the decisions about the Growth and Development of the Institution, it's Vision and Mission.

Problem Solving Decisions

A number of problems do arise in every system. An effective and dynamic Principal is able to resolve them. There are the problems of the staff, students and other stake holders. There can be group conflicts, disorders, disturbances, clashes and many other problems. Following the processes mentioned below will help in problem solving ..

Identifying and defining the problem.

Fnding and examining the facts.

Consulting and involving others.

Deciding course of action.

Evaluating the results.

An efficient Principal decides ' What is Wrong not Who is Wrong.'

Action Taking

Principal is the supreme authority in the Institution. Actions as deemed fit need to be taken in the larger interest of Institution.In absence of timely and proper actions the smooth functioning may adversely be affected. Sometimes Punitive as well as Corrective actions are must against the defaulters, shirkers, poor performers, arrogants and indisciplined employees.

Remember every action will have a reaction. Man with dual mind is really blind.

Action taking is rather a difficult and harder process. It is always suggested to adopt the Corrective measures to control the behavior and mend the ways.

Actions should speak louder than the words. Stringent actions must be taken against the people for dereliction of duties.

When our Actions are based on good Intentions, our soul has no regrets.

Controlling

Principal is the Principal Controller in the Institution exercising control over each and every aspect. Every aspect of the Institution must be within the reach and grip of the Principal. Principal is also the Quality Controller, ensures quality functioning, Quality Education and accordingly sets goals/standards.

For an efficient administration and management the Principal must possess both Hard and Soft Skills.

Hard Skills

- Essential and Desirable Qualifications,
- Experience.
- Training.

Soft Skills

- Personality.
- Values.
- Attitude.
- Behaviour

An ideal principal should be able to change Institution's Narratives by Skilling self and others and further by Re-skilling and Up-skilling.

CHAPTER V

Principal as a Leader – Leadership Skills

There is now a paradigm shift from BOSSING to MANAGING and MANAGING to LEADING. Most appropriate word for the Head of Institution is now a LEADER.

Who is a Leader?

In common language Leader is one who Knows the way, Shows the Way and Goes the Way. Knows the way means has the knowledge of the system, its Mission, Vision, rules and regulations. Shows the way means Guides the fellow employees , motivates them. Goes The way is to set examples and become their Role Model .

Leader is one who is an efficient and effective performer, guides, motivates, builds teams for smooth functioning, is a catalyst, and brings positive changes in the Organization.

Leader is one who is Result Driven, Eager to learn, Innovative, confident, Hard Working,. Emphatic and Trust Worthy.

<u>Leader is one who has in abundance the following qualities</u>
The Ability to Dream

- Physical as well as Mental Courage.
- Adherence to Discipline.
- Willing to Sacrifice
- Unquestionable Integrity.

Principal is the Leader of the Institution he heads, Leads the staff and students to realize The Vision and Mission of the Organization. The Institution can become a Learning Organization only when the Leader is Effective and Dynamic. Principal as a Leader has to be Effective both as a Person as well as a Professional.

Leadership is influencing the people to strive Willingly to accomplish the desired objectives. Effective Leadership will certainly create an environment where all Stakeholders feel that they are very much part and partial of the Organization. Good Leader will allow them to participate wholeheartedly and contribute significantly. Good Leadership will eradicate all barriers and obstacles in the growth of the Institution.

> *"Leaders do not conform, they reform.*
> *'If you Conform, you are nurturing Mediocrity. If you Reform, you are breeding change.'*
>
> *-Israelmore Ayier."*

Strong Leaders do not put others down but they lift them up. Followers never know how hard the Leader tries to create a path.Leader has to wear many hats. Good Leaders don't create followers but they create Leaders.

> *"Most people think Leadership as a Position and therefore don't see themselves as Leaders.*
>
> *-Stephen Covey."*

Talents are required to be a Leader. In fact leaders don't act, they fix goals and make others achieve them. Leaders are their own Role Models. They are Catalysts.

Leadership is a charisma

Great Leaders are always in a hurry. The perspectives of good Leaders are broad not narrow. A Principal as a Leader must know and understand that the secrets of success are

- **Passion.**
- **Conviction.**
- **Commitment.**
- **Devotion.**

Remember this must become Principal's Dossier. The potentials and initiatives of the Principal as a Leader can yield desired results.

Leadership Qualities of Principal

Ability to be a Catalyst. Principal has to be a Change Agent.

Must also be able to manage the change.

Ability to Inspire and persuade.

The Principal's inspiration and ability to persuade the team helps in following

the righteous path to accomplish the tasks and achieve the results.

Principal as a Leader puts the ideas into people's minds and inspires them to work.

Ability to Empower

Empowering the followers is one of the greatest qualities of a leader. Team can not perform unless it feels empowered.

Ability to Perform

Good leader is a performer. Institution's success depends on the performance of the Principal. Performance leads to recognition, recognition leads to respect and respect leads to power. Therefore, performance is key to success.

Perform or Perish is the main Mantra.

Ability to craft a great Vision

An effective Leader is a Visionary. He/ she has the ability to articulate it and raise the aspirations, confidence, pride, hope and enthusiasm of the people.

Ability to Motivate

Motivation is a great source of performance. Principal ought to motivate the staff and students to perform and grow. Good leaders not only motivate but always ensure that people don't feel demotivated in any circumstances.

"Remember Motivation comes from our minds while Inspiration comes from our hearts."

Role Modeling

The Principal as a Leader must become the role model for the subordinates. Must be able to set examples. It is very easy to give examples but at the same time not so easy to become an example.

Leading from the Front.

Leader's main role is to lead. Leading the team to accomplish objectives of the Organization.It is not to lead only but to lead from the front. Leader is first everywhere, always on the forefront.

Risk Bearing.

It is rightly said' **No Risk no Gain.'**

Principal as a leader has to bear the risk and uncertainties to succeed. These risks can be pertaining to certain Decisions and Actions about Academics, Administration, Finances. Principal must be competent enough to put his view before the concerned authorities.

<u>**Five Cs to lead without a title**</u>

"*Be Courageous.*

Courage is the backbone of Leadership. Leaders must have the courage to function openly and take difficult decisions and actions.

Be Contagious.

Must leave an impact and legacy behind.

Be Communicative.

Leaders must be able to communicate in simple, clear and understandable language.

Be Collaborative.

Must have a collaborative approach, taking all along and functioning with consultation.

Be Caring.

Leader is the guardian of the team. Must be able to take care of all concerned."

Remember **K A I Z E N** i.e. better than before. Functioning of all affairs better than before.

Leadership Styles

<u>**Most common Leadership Styles are:**</u>

1. Autocratic Style

Such leaders centralize power with themselves. The subordinates do what they are told to do. Leadership behavior is based on threat and punishment. **They believe in Monologue rather than Dialogue.**

2. Participative Style.

Such Leaders decentralize the authority and believe in Collaboration.They trust the team are trustworthy. This is the best style.

Discussion is an exchange of Thoughts and Knowledge. Promote it.

Argument is an exchange of ego and arrogance. Avoid it.

Discussion enables Learning, Argument may lead to misunderstandings.

3. Free Rein Style.

Such Leaders avoid power and responsibilities. Leader plays a minor role and all major roles are given to others. They fail to guide and motivate.

This is the era of discussions, Collaboration, participation and Interactions.

Principal as a Leader has, therefore, Multidimensional Roles and tremendous responsibilities. There are several examples of the **Principals who rose to prominence due their concerted and sustained efforts, sheer dedication and discipline in their personal as well as Professional lives.**

CHAPTER VI

Principal as a Person

Don't let your tongue cut your throat.

Before being an Academician, Administrator, Manager and Leader, Principal is a person. The pleasing personally of Principal, both his/her exterior and interior not only attract one and all but leave an everlasting impact on them. Not necessarily a good person will be an effective academician, administrator, manager or leader. It depends on how the Principal is able to acquire the knowledge, hone skills and possess a learning attitude.

Once somebody told Pascal , " **If I had your brain, I would have been a much better person.**" Pascal replied, " **First you be a better person then you can have my brain.**"

Hence to become an effective and dynamic professional, one has to be a good person.Principal derives power from his personality and position, known as...

Personal Power and Positional Power.

These days we may have good academicians, administrators, managers and leaders but very difficult to find a good human being. The main reason is absence of values, mannerism, positivity and affinity.

Once a man with a lantern in his hand was was searching something in broad day light on the streets of Athens. The passers by were surprised on seeing this. A man asked him,"What are you searching and why with a lantern in day light?" " I searched throughout night also but could not find. Even now I am unable to find." replied the man. "In fact I am searching for a good human being."

There are two important powers with every person as a professional...

Personal Power.

On top of all, Principal is a person. The personality traits, attributes and characteristics of Principal contribute significantly to his/her success. A negative or a bad person can never become a good professional. Therefore, the principal has to be..

Humble ... Doesn'ttreat himself as very important. A respectful person polite in nature.

Docile... peaceful, quiet and calm. An obedient person. Easy to be understood. Not very talkative.

Gentle... Not keeping any grudges against any one. By and large kind and soft spoken. These qualities make principal a gentleman.

Submissive....Listens to all, orderly, kind hearted. Submits self for the cause of others.

Considerate.. Empathetic,considers the requests of others, a favourable attitude.

Concerned... Every affair of the Institution must be the serious concern of the Principal. **Unconcerrned** behaviour may cause disaster. Caring nature benefits self as well as others.

'Care is most beautiful word which makes life richer. If someone tells you take care, that means you live in their hearts.'

Cooperative...The helping hand and cooperative nature of the Principal not only wins the hearts but also lead to Institutional development.

Positive. Always believes self and thinks positive about others. Constructive approach.

Positive thinkers have a solution for every problem. Negative thinkers have problem for every solution.

These are not merely the attributes but also the requirements of the job.

Positional Power..

A person's most beautiful asset is not head full of knowledge but heart full of love, an ear ready to listen and a hand willing to help.

Positional Power comes from the authority granted to the Principal. The Principal has the power to take decisions and actions . He has the authority to mend the ways of subordinates by the prescribed rules and regulations, has the power to direct and control.

There are the Principals who use more of their Positional Power than that of Personal Power and some otherwise. But Research says that an effective Principal is one who uses more of personal power and less of positional power. The percentage is 70 and 30 respectively.

Further for being a good person the Principal must remember that:

Warm hospitality and insightful conversation builds healthy relations.

Soft attitude creates strong relations.

A good person and an efficient professional always follows one's passion and never loses focus.

Be proactive and not reactive.

Expressive not aggressive.

Affiliative not subtle.

The importance of good people is just like the importance of heart beat. It is not visible but silently supports our life.

Principal has to be a person with sterling qualities.

Remember that there is no short cut to success. Short cut leads to Short Circuit. All great achievers are the products of adversity and not of facility.

"*Smaller deeds done are better than great deeds planned.*"

CHAPTER VII

Guiding Principles – Personal Principles

This is the era of Principle Centered Leadership. There are certain guiding Principles in absence of which the Leaders can not achieve the Organizational Goals. These Principles not only guide about the right and wrong but also prescribe a code of conduct for both persons and Professionals.

What are the Principles?

Principles are certain guiding rules or laws directing the individuals to follow the correct path. These are the fundamental ideals or beliefs of moral code based on assumptions. These principles certainly gude as well as direct one and all about the right direction to be followed.

These Principles can be categorized as under..

Individual/Personal Principles.

Moral Principles.

Professional Principles

Leadership Principles.

A person with principles is always able to regulate his behavior as well as action which ultimately leads to success in every sphere. Principles not only develop the personality and build character of a person but are also essential tools for the congenial environment of the organization.

The ability of the Principal to cherish the values and Principles upholded by great people will add another feather in his cap. Strong value base and Principles Centred Leadership can result in spectacular progress and Success.

Some of the personal principles are listed below..

1. **Principle of Simplicity..**

Life is really Simple. But we insist on making it complicated. Confucius.

Simplicity is a personal value. It doesn't mean ordinary or narrow thinking. It is about the Principal's attributes. It should reflect in one's nature, behaviour and action. The functioning and communication of the Principal should be so simple that everyone is able to grasp and comprehend. Complicated handling never yields better results. **Simple Living and High Thinking is a success mantra.**

Simplicitymakes life peaceful, joyful andblissful. Free yourself from the complexities of life. Peace is a Fundamental Value. A peaceful mind leads to peaceful functioning.

'There is no way of peace. Peace is the way. If peace is the goal, how can war be the way'?

M K Gandhi.

2.Principle of Sincerity..

A **sincere person is one who understands his duties and responsibilities.** Such a person is good at heart, devoted and genuine. The subordinates learn a lot from a sincere person. Value base of a sincere person is automatically strong. It is a behavioural trait and such a person is never hurting. It is always true that for smooth functioning **we don't need serious leaders but sincere leaders.** Sincere Principal is reliable and trustworthy. Such people neither pretend nor deceive.

3.Principle of Self-awareness..

Speak a line to yourself everyday..

I **am the best. I can do it. God is always with me.I am a winner.Today is my day. Dr. A P J Kalam.**

Knowing and understanding yourself is perhaps the greatest quality of a person. The Principal being Head of the Institution must be able to recognize self. If a person fails to know the self will not be able to understand others. Self awareness is one of the important life skills.

Self awareness is all about observing and recognizing oneself , knowing relationships amongst thoughts, feelings, actions and reactions.

Talk to yourself at least once a day otherwise you may miss meeting an excellent person in life.

You can not believe in God unless you believe in yourself.

4.Principle of Self Discipline..

Discipline is control over personal whims, impulses and desires. It is obedience to prescribed Code of Conduct involving certain restrictions. It is a valuable asset. Discipline is essential to ensure individual freedom.These days discipline is treated as a threat to individual freedom especially by the youngsters. But it is the most important component of organised civil life.

Discipline grows from within and not from without. Principal has to be a disciplined person. Self discipline is key to success. If the principal himself is not disciplined, he/she can never maintain discipline in others.

Self discipline is about controlling and regulating self. To discipline oneself one has to develop good habits and these habits gradually lead to self acceptance which lays the foundation of success. A self disciplined person is always a satisfied person and is able to accomplish the objectives.

5.Principle of Empathy...

Empathy is the cognitive ability to understand others feelings. It is putting yourself in others' position , a deep and sincere concern for others. It is expected that the Principal should not only be sympathetic but empathetic. It is one of the greatest qualities of a top line manager. One can be empathetic by showing serious concern, sharing, listening actively, recognizing, helping and always coming forward to solve problems of others/fellow colleagues.

An empathetic person is not only concerned but also considerate. They are not only better persons but better professionals as well. They have the attitude of gratitude and never feel pride in providing a helping hand.

Empathy and Compassion are the need of the hour. The empathetic approach of the Principal will automatically solve a number of problems of the Institution. It can be **Cognitive ie,**

intelligent enough to sense the feelings of others. Emotional ie sentimental towards others and Compassionate ie desirous to help.

Empathy plays a key role in building human relations. It has two parts, the ability to recognize another person's thoughts and feelings and the ability to respond with an appropriate emotion. The first part is called 'Cognitive Empathy' and the second 'Affective Empathy'.

6.Principle of Forgiveness..

A Long Lasting Relationship comes with a lot of Forgiveness and Understanding.

It **is often said, forget and forgive the petty issues, deeds. Forgiveness is not to have a resentful approach.** This quality is not good for others but also for self also. It reduces anxiety, stress, misunderstandings of both, the forgiven and the forgiver. It is not very easy to forgive, one has to compromise on several fronts and prepare accordingly. Emotions need to be controlled, needs patience, time to think and courage. It is not overlooking the work and conduct . It is also not for the mistakes committed intentionally. .It is a thought provoking and psychological process but very useful for building healthy and cordial relations. But the person forgiven must be advised to be particular in future and not to repeat the same. Forgiving for the right cause boosts morale and enhances efficiency.

Remember too much Analysis leads to paralysis. Most easy and difficult things in life are two, mistakes easy to judge when others do it and difficult to assess when we commit them.

Forgiveness has always been helpful in building healthy, strong, stable and good relations. A long lasting relationship comes with a lot of forgiveness.

7.Principle of Happiness..

Happiness is the best Destination.It is the costliest thing in the world.

Happiness is a state of mind. It is the best immunity booster. It is a state of mind, priceless and also free. If you ever have a chance to make someone happy just avail this opportunity. We should never regret a bad day in our life. It is very correctly said that good days give happiness, bad days give experiences, the worst day gives lessons and the best days give memories.A happy and cheerful Principal is always able to enhance the happiness index of subordinates.

Happiness in fact is not a goal, it is a journey. There is no path to happiness, happiness is a path itself. One can be cheerful if he/she is able to cheer someone else. Happiness fosters WE feelings and thus good for organizational hygiene.

Remember the beautiful thing in the world is to see a smiling person and the most beautiful thing is when you are behind it.

Similarly many other Personal Principles play a dominant role in succes of a person and organisation. Some of these are Principles of Humility, Compassion, Fairness, Righteous Conduct , magnanimity, tolerance, gratitude, determination etc.

Happy employees work harder or otherwise employees will work hard but without gratitude. Therefore, the Principal has to be happy himself and happily guide, help, protect them.

The Happiness Index of the Institution should be very high. Higher the happiness the better will be the performance and productivity. **Happiness is not a goal, it is a journey. Love others and promote WE feelings. You can be happy by becoming a better person and not by possessions.**

To be happy we must have firm belief in reality. Realists are happier than the optimists.

Remember laughter is the Best Medicine. Exchange of pleasantries make people happy.

8.Principle of Healthy Living..

Health is not just about what you are eating. It is also about what you are thinking and saying.

Health is wealth and Healthy mind in Healthy body are very popular slogans. Without a healthy lifestyle we can not maintain good health. In absence of good health we can not contribute to the fullest of our capabilities. The person in charge of the entire

Institution has to be **physically, mentally, emotionally and spiritually healthy.** The principal can not be an able Administrator, effective Manager, Efficient Academician and Innovative Leader unless his/her health status is good.

Healthy living is a habit. It is our responsibility and completely in our hands. *According to Spiritual Guru Sri Sri Ravishankar, ' Your Body is Your Life Partner. Always stays with you. The more you care for your body the more your body will care for you. It is your most valuable asset or otherwise can become the biggest liability for you.'*

Principal should not only look healthy but also cultivate a healthy lifestyle. Being a role model for students and teachers, they will certainly emolute.

It is not important how long we live but most important is how well we live. Add meaning to your life each day.

8.Principle of Maturity...

Maturity is generally related to age. But in professional terms it is about matured behaviour. Sometimes the professionals may not demonstrate a matured behavior or maturity is not reflected in their words and actions. Therefore, the Principal being Head of the Institution must always display maturity in administrative and managerial affairs. A **matured person talks sense, he is emotionally stable and his decisions and actions will speak of his maturity.**

9.Principle of Spirituality..

Spirituality is not necessarily being religious.

A spiritual person is not one who has blind faith in god, religion or one who is an orthodox.

It is our connection with our soul. Those who understand self and others are spiritual. A spiritual person knows and understands that there is definitely someone over and above self who is supreme and controls our actions and keeps us away from wrong deeds. **Empathy, intelligence, wisdom, understanding, love, peace, truth all are our spiritual powers.** Principal holding the highest and very important position, has to be spiritual to set the examples for others.

The above principles strengthen the Principal and enable him to build a very meticulous and impregnable system which everyone would like to join, perform and grow.

32

CHAPTER VIII

Moral Principles

You must remember that some things that are legally right may not be morally right. Abraham Lincoln.

Principal is not only the Head of the Institution but also responsible for shaping the personality of the students and building their character. It is possible only when the Principal himself/herself is the person of morals and character. Moral means righteous behavior, conduct and action. A person of morality is able to identify and distinguish between right and wrong, understands what is to be done and not to be done. It is a quality of being right.

Although practising moral principles is essential everywhere but more important in Educational Institutions where the future of the nation is prepared.

Morality is identified with ethics and symbolizes right and wrong. Whatever is right or just and within the principles promoting social good can not be immoral.Moral way of life is good mannerism, following accepted code of conduct, a set of beliefs, what is good, having understanding of desirable and praiseworthy issues. Moral Education is of course part and partial of the curriculum.

Some of the Moral Principles are discussed below...

1.Honesty

> *"Honesty is the first chapter in the book of Wisdom.*
> *-Thomas Jefferson"*

Honesty is freedom from deceit , being true to self and others. It is a value which filters down from top to bottom. If the Principal is honest, it leaves an impact on all others . Principal should not appear to be honest but has truly be honest. As the saying goes, **'Honesty is the best Policy'**, but at the same time it is a virtue by itself which ought to be cultivated and should be observed everywhere. Honesty is being true to oneself and dishonesty is cheating oneself. Different aspects of honesty can be observed at home, in social places and at work. An honest person is an asset to the organization. It benefits the person concerned as well as the entire system. Such a person is dependable and trustworthy. Straightforwardness, commitment, loyalty, and positivity are some other qualities.

> *"'Chanakya was the great Indian strategist and Guru of governance, one of the foremost proponents of ethical behavior of the king. Once Chanakya was busy with official work. A Chinese visitor came to him for some advice. He put off the burning lamp and lit another lamp before starting the conversation. The curious visitor asked him about this action. Chanakya replied that he was doing some state work and therefore, used the official lamp. But now we are busy with the personal work, therefore, I lit the personal lamp'."*

See the degree of Honesty.
Greed is like sea water, the more we drink the thirstier we get.
2. Integrity

> *"What you think you become, what you feel you attract, what you imagine you create. -Buddha.*
> *"*

It refers to undoubted identity, free from all sorts of corruption and very high on morality. It is excellent and dignified conduct, strong value base and sound character. In public life integrity is the highest quality of one's conduct. A person of undoubted integrity is always free from false pride and thus known for his outstanding contribution to the propagation of **Transparency, Accountability and Sincerity.**

The Principal being Head of the Institution must be a person of Unquestioned Integrity. Then only the Principal can set the example and become a Role Model for the students and Faculty. But it does not mean that the Principal should be high on moral grounds and low on understanding. The amicable and intelligible behavior leaves an indelible impact on every mind. Person of undisputed integrity does not expect any favour from anywhere, is honourable, truthful and trustworthy. He/she is always positive and understands that weakness of attitude become the weakness of Character.

Person of integrity abides by law, never misuses power and position.

3.Truthfulness

Truth is one of the Fundamental Values. It is a firm belief in truths, facts and reality. It is the quality of one's character and behavior. A truthful person is one who is not only true to his words but action and decisions also. Truth is our biggest support and plays an important role in the success of the person as well as the Organization. It is the basis of all Human Relations.

All religions preach and teach the same truth, maybe in different manners. All the things in and around us are real hence their existence is true. Our life experiences, sweet or sour, are also true. Having faith in all realities is the truth.

A true person succeeds in all his endeavors and becomes an example for others. Truthfulness is therefore, one of the greatest qualities of human behaviour. Truth builds confidence and confidence leads to success.

4.Justice

Justice is the charity of a wise man. It is nothing else but true freedom.

Justice is a fair and impartial approach towards the decisions and actions. Principal must be a judicious person treating and behaving with all in a similar manner. If a top line manager is fair and just, the subordinates are likely to be fair in their work and conduct. An unfair leader harms himself as well as the organization. Impartial approach inspires and motivates the teachers and taught.

It is **moral righteousness.** The principal has to do justice with self, with job and the stakeholders. All look forward to the Principal for seeking justice directly or indirectly. Justice is said to have been done if appropriate and acceptable decisions are taken, conflicts are amicably resolved, problems are judiciously solved and the subordinates are persuaded properly.

While maintaining discipline and following the code of conduct the Principal has to mend the ways of faculty and students, reprimand/punishment is essential . If they are able to improve and do not repeat the same, Retributive justice has been done. Similarly, Corrective justice is done to correct the people in their attitude and behaviour.

Principal has to be very cautious while doing justice. Equity, equality, fairness and transparency are the factors to be considered. Justice delayed is justice denied. Hence timely justice is of great importance.

The Principle of Natural Justice is more important in Administration. Several judgements are also passed on the basis of Natural Justice. It is to provide sufficient time to be heard to the justice seeker. No biased decision is to be taken.

Dispensation of justice should be felt by all. Therefore, the Principal has to ensure that justice done to one doesn't become injustice to others. One must not display any prejudices and always follow the principles of equity, justice and mutual respect.

5.Loyalty

It **is about our commitments to the organization. This is the quality of our character and a human value.** Loyalty is the gratefulness to the Institution that we are serving. Any person who is deeply involved, fully committed and treats the Institution as own family, free from any greed and selfishness is a loyal person. One has to be loyal to self, family, friends and the system. It is in fact a sense of allegiance to the system.

It **is about the belongingness to the Institution you are heading. In** an Educational Institution where not only the education is imparted but values are imbibed, personality is developed, character is built, loyalty is much more important.

We must always remember and understand the contribution of the organization in our personal growth in terms of pay, perks, facilities, promotions and capacity building. At the same time we must also assess our contribution towards the growth and development of the organization. If so we are loyal otherwise not.

It is expected that the Principal being the Father figure should be able to develop this sense of ownership and faithfulness amongst the staff and students by being loyal to himself/herself.

CHAPTER IX

Professional Principles

Principal is the Professional that too of a Noble Profession. There are certain Professional beliefs, ideals and Ethics that the Principal has to embrace.

Professionalism of Principle must be visible in every affair of the Institution.Principal is a professional because he/she possesses all soft as well hard skills to guide and inspire the teachers and taught.

Principal is the professional involved in a very important activity i.e. making and shaping the personality of students who in turn will become the professionals in various fields. Principal must possess professional ethics such as honesty, integrity, responsibility, morality etc. These professional ethics are very essential to accomplish the objectives of the Institution. A professional has to be normally sound, physically and mentally strong and self motivated.

The basis of the Professional Principles is Professional Ethics consisting of honesty, integrity, confidentiality , morality, discipline etc. Principal should be a pioneer of ethics.

Professional Principles can be discussed as under:

1. Competence

Competency is the first and foremost trait of a professionals. Competency is the ability to perform the assigned job. An incompetent person does not deserve to be called a professional. Competence is to possess all the skills and capabilities to administer, manage and lead. It may not relate to a single individual but also to a group, team or the entire organisation.

Competence leads to Excellence. Excellence can be achieved not by competing with others but by competing with self. Every Institution strives for excellence in education. Principal's initiatives will be supported and cooperated only when there exists an environment of trust and good Interpersonal relationship.

Outstanding and inspiring contribution of every stakeholder, their massive participation will be instrumental to strengthen the sense of responsibility and realising the objectives. The Institution can thus emerge as the most cherished centre of Excellence.

Relentless efforts of the Principal, faculty and students give them more strength to meet the challenges and setbacks in way of achieving Excellence. More and more avenues need to be explored.

Who is a competent person?

One who is capable enough to undertake, assess and complete the assigned task successfully. A set of knowledge, skills and abilities are also required. **Your core competencies also include your walk, talk, behaviour, actions and decisions. A** competent person is efficient, effective and able to make judicious decisions. A competent Principal is able to build the Institution a Learning Organization where an excellent academic environment prevails, teaching learning is innovative, known for its discipline and high and healthy traditions.

Managerial, behavioural, technological and conceptual skills along with a variety of abilities, general awareness, common sense, knowledge, habits, values and attitude are the indicators of a person's Competence.

. A competent Principal understands the system, its policies, objectives, procedures, is technology savvy and gets the work done at the right time by the right people.

Main source of competence is Knowledge. Unless the Principal has thorough knowledge of the processes, procedures, policies and organizational structure, the objectives of growth and development can not be achieved. There is no limit to acquiring knowledge. Human mind is so fertile and capable of retaining it and is never full.

' **A man used to beg on a busy street of a city. The people generously poured money into his bowl. Once a passerby asked the beggar,' your bowl is never full in spite of so much pouring'. 'My bowl is made of human skull, hence never full'. Replied the** beggar.

2. Confidence

Confidence is to have full faith in one's knowledge and abilities to perform a particular job. A confident person is sure to be successful while performing. Self confidence is a personality trait. But at the same time overconfidence is always harmful and threatening. If a person trusts self and the team the results are wonderful and encouraging.

Principal of the Institution is expected to be confident about achieving good results, creating congenial and cordial relations, and accomplishing the vision and mission of the Organization. Besides, confidence in the team is also equally important.

IfLeader is filled with courage and confidence, the impossible can also be achieved.

3. Commitment

It is the belongingness and ownership towards the Institution being headed. Any person deserves to be called a professional only when he/she is fully devoted and committed to the system, treats the Institution as own enterprise and desists from anti organization practices. Always takes initiatives, works with full captivity and capability to yield desired results. Pledges himself to the organization, reaffirms self to take the Institution to the highest level.

Initiations and Consistency are two important factors to fulfill our commitment to the Organization. Commitment is helpful in developing work culture and motivating the team. Commitment building is an important function of HR managers. The indicators of Commitment are high spirits, zeal, enthusiasm, involvement and trust. The commitment is beyond pays, perks, promotions, rewards and recognitions.

Commitment comes from Hard work and determination. Hard work never goes in vain.

In Ramayana Jatayu the vulture told Rama about Sita. Hanuman was given the task to discover Sita. After several efforts Hanuman gave up the hope to discover. He thought that

Rama, Laxman and Sugrive will die of sorrow. Hanuman wanted to commit suicide. While busy in these thoughts, Hanuman saw a small Bird taking flight towards the ocean again and again. Sipping some water and throwing it out of mouth. This act was being repeated again and again. Hanuman asked the reason. ' I want to dry up the ocean because my nest fell in it' Hanuman got inspiration and found Sita.

4. Effectiveness

A competent person may not always be an Effective Person. Effectiveness is a skill to influence the staff and students and leave an ever lasting impact on them. Such person is self motivated and activates and energises everyone to deliver their best. *Harnessing the collective individuality, being proactive, goal and result oriented, fully determined, fixing priorities are some of the indicators of Effectiveness.*

5. Responsibility

Liberty means Responsibility. That is why most men dread it. G B. Shaw.

Responsibility is being answerable and acceptable. It is to ensure that the system being headed is functioning smoothly and judiciously. Duties are being discharged with commitment and Integrity. *One must accept responsibility for actions and must be accountable for results.* One has to be responsible to self, family and all the stake holders in the system.

Responsibility is not only towards the assigned tasks ie the professional responsibility but it can also be moral, social and legal as well.

6. Reliability

Professional growth depends on the Principle of Reliability. A Principal as a Professional must be reliable and trustworthy. A reliable person can significantly contribute to the organisational growth.Reliable person is good performer as he/ she is able to build confidence and competence in a team, can win their faith and support and becomes the Trend Setter.

Building Relationships..

Principal is also a Relationship Manager. The smooth functioning of an Institution is directly dependent on Healthy Relations. It is the Professional calibre of the Principal to build and maintain good relationships amongst all the stakeholders. The cordial relation between Principal, staff, students, , patents and community are of great importance for the progress of the Institution.

Sweetest relations are like pillows, when you're tired you relax on them. When you're sad you drop tears on them. When you are angry, you punch them and when you are happy you hug them.

The Principal has to ensure a healthy environment in the Institution in order to build good relationships. Poor relations not only create misunderstandings but also several hindrances in the system.All beautiful relations don't depend on how well you understand others but depend on how well you manage the misunderstandings.

Honest Relations ate just like water, no colour, no shape and no taste but still very important for survival.

Distance never kills relations, closeness never builds relations. It is the care of someone's feelings which builds faith and maintains relations.

Treat your money and relations with equal respect because both are hard to make and easy to lose. Success and relationship never depend on the capability of your brain, rather depend on the greatness of your behaviour and thoughts. Listen to everyone and learn from everyone. **Nobody knows everything but everybody knows something.**

A long lasting Relationship comes with a lot of forgiveness and understanding.Most important formula of success is knowing how to deal with people.Principal's focus on people is very important to build relationships. People don't care how much you know until they know how much you care for them.

Furthermore, the Principal has to be particular about the following to develop a good relationship..

- Never underestimate your subordinates.
- Be considerate,
- Ask for their advice
- Be good listener.
- Let them feel important.
- Avoid Arguments.

CHAPTER X

Leadership Principles

Leadership is Fighting all odds, overcoming challenges and emerging as a Winner .

Leadership qualities are inherent in every individual, degrees vary. Some people assume naturally, whereas some have to make conscious efforts to evolve as a leader. School is the best platform to develop Leadership Qualities. Students learn to be responsible, gather confidence, become courageous, develop the attitude of sharing and caring and team spirit. Family, work place, experience, attitude, behaviour are also very essential contributors.

Leader of the Institution is the Principal and Principal's Personality reflects in it.If the Principal is able to deliver effectively, persuades them to work together willingly, he deserves to be called a Leader.

Leadership is an outstanding aspect of management. It manifests ability ,creativity,Initiative and innovation. Leader is an influencing **person having all Human, Technical, Conceptual and Behavioral Skills.**

Principal along with the teachers must make serious and sincere efforts to imbibe the spirit of 'Learners today, Leaders Tomorrow.'

The attributes of Leadership must percolate down to the subordinates. Farsighted and vibrant leadership is able to impress upon all others. Indelible contribution of a leader is very much visible in the functioning of the Institution.

There are numerous Leadership Principles. Prominent of them are appended below..

1.Vision and Mission..

Poor eyes limit you sight, Poor VISION limits your Dreams. *Franklin Field.*

Vision is a picture in our mind's eye about the prospects of the Organization in future.It is ability to visualize the future, Core values and purpose of the organization. It is constructing an envisioned future. It is not prediction but the Leader's commitments for future Accomplishments. Vision Statement is to be displayed properly and has to be communicated to all stakeholders.

Vision is a dream with dead lines, forward thinking. It is to look beyond the present and to see what the future can be. A vision Statement clarifies what the Institution can be at its best .

Greater the Vision, greater the potentials it creates. It opens doors of opportunities for growth and development.

Mission is the conversion of vision into reality. The Principal has to be a Missionary having zeal and enthusiasm to achieve the Aims and Objectives of the Institution. The mission should be realistic and achievable. Principal must plan proper strategies to accomplish the Mission.

Fear always stands in the way of fulfilling a Mission. Therefore, the mission has to be achieved without fear. An efficient Principal is always able to fulfill the resolutions proposed.

Shared Vision is the common view of the team about the future of the Organization. When the picture of the organization about its future prospects is similar in the eyes and mind of the stakeholders, it forms a shared vision. Any Institution functioning with the similar vision in mind can grow at an alarming rate and the achievements will be credible. Shared Vision develops a sense of ownership towards the Institution, builds trust and enhances team spirit. The leader creates vision and shares with the followers in order to form Shared Vision.

A **commendable crafted vision takes the Institution to its highest level.** It can showcase qualitative and praise worthy achievements.

Mission clarifies how the Institutional Goals can be achieved or in other words how to accomplish the Vision of the Institution. It is an action oriented expression. The clear explanation of this

is known as Mission Statement. It mainly specifies the Purpose of the Organization.

Mission Statement should be...

- Motivational and Emotional.
- Easily understandable and Transformable.
- Attainable.
- Simple and Honest.
- Fully Trusted.

Vision and Mission both aim at:
Generating energy and Enthusiasm amongst the employees.
Fixing the Goals and strategies to accomplish them.
Enhancement of commitment and confidence.
Creating a sense of ownership and Responsibility.
Vision without Mission is incomplete and Mission without Vision is of no meaning.
2.Motivation
A self motivated Leader can only motivate others. It is an internal urge and spirit within self to get the job done. Principal has to be a self motivated person and capable enough to motivate others. People feel motivated only when the work culture is cordial and congenial. The motivational forces of every member of the Institution must be tapped properly. People in any organization are most important assets. They need inspiration and morale boosting from time to time.

Capability to work and desire to work are different. Motivation helps to enhance both. Motivation is an act of stimulating oneself and someone to work efficiently and effectively. **It is to press the right button to achieve the desired results.** It is a psychological concept related to operating forces within the employees. It is a continuous process. Principal is the right person to undertake this important activity in the Institution.

If the Principal is competent enough to motivate the staff and students, the institution will have the following advantages ....

Kindling the desire to work.

Development of a sense of responsibility.

Discipline among the staff and students.

Maximum utilisation of resources.

Enhancement in efficiency and productivity.

Fosters morality and loyalty.

Motivation can either be positive or negative. Rewards and incentives are forms of positive motivation whereas punishment/ reprimands is negative motivation. Principal has to adopt both the meausers of motivation.

According to eminent psychologist Abraham Mashlow people feel motivated only when their prominent needs are satisfied. These are self actualisation, esteem, social safety and physiological needs. Principal has to take care of all these needs of the students and staff to motivate them.

Principal is the prime motivator in the Institution. In order to motivate the Principal has to ascertain ....

What makes the employee perform better.

What keeps them contented.

What will help them to stay in the Institution.

3.Communication

Communication is the lifeline of any relation. When you stop communcating, you start losing your valuable relations.

Communication is one of the dominating processes in Leadership. Effective communication both oral and written is of paramount importance in leadership. Principal must be expert in this art of transmitting information, ideas, opinion, facts from one person to another/group.

This is the process of sharing information through various sources with the team as words, letters, symbols etc. Must be known for his oratory skills, noting and drafting. This quality impresses and influences all. Most of the problems occur due to communication gap and misunderstandings.

In an Educational Institution communication is more important because the quality of instructions, institutional management, discipline, interpersonal relations are directly dependent on Effective Combination.

4.Trust

'A bird sitting on the branch of a tree has no fear of falling not because the branch is solid but because it has faith in its wings.'

Principal must have trust in self and his team and expected to make sincere efforts to become **Trustworthy. Trust is the soul of Leadership. Without trust every word is misunderstood,*with trust even silence is understood.*** Trust is to have full confidence and faith in team members, their potentials and integrity. Trust is the reliability of Leader on the subordinates. Commitment, dedication and honesty towards duties and responsibilities are the strongest contributors of Trust Building.

TR U S T can be expanded as under...

T.... It is about truths and facts. To have trust in followers and become Trustworthy. One has to be true to words and action.

R.... It is Responsibility towards a task. Trust can not be built without the sense of Responsibility ie accepting the responsibility wholeheartedly.

U...It is unity, for trust building, the entire Institution is a unit and all functionaries are a Team. They sail together.

T....It is Teamwork. Effective functioning and Trusting Relationships take the Institution very far.

Mistrust creates suspicion and hostility which is fatal for Institutional growth.

Faith is a small word but has supreme implications. People have doubts in their faith and have full faith in their doubts.

5.Accountability..

It **is over and above Responsibility. Responsibility can be collective but Accountability is Individual.** Accountability is owning the responsibility. It is the sense of belongingness for a particular outcome. Accountability is what the leader is supposed to accomplish with fair means. Accountability is an internal aspect of leadership, ie the Leader feels from his core of heart about the achievements and accomplishments. Responsibility can be understood but accountability is felt. It is one's commitment towards achievements.

Accountability is an Attitude and for the Leader it should become a habit. Accountability is fulfilling the expectations and aspirations of self and others. Blame games are hazardous for accountability. The leader must accept the failures. The subordinates can be held responsible for under achievements but the Principal is accountable. In fact Responsibility leads to Accountability. One who doesn't feel responsibility can never be accountable.

Managing the Change

A Catalyst

> *"The measure of intelligence is ability to change.*
>
> *-Albert Einstein."*

The Principal being the Leader of the Institution is the Change Agent and plays role of a catalyst. Change is a Transitional process of Transforming and Empowering the Faculty. The Principal should do away with old and obsolete methodology and introduce modern innovative and multidisciplinary approaches to achieve the objectives. The changes can be in Processes, Procedures, Equipments, Technology, Methodology Culture etc.

Principal has to prepare the stakeholders to adapt and accept the change. Change is accepted only when it is properly planned, implemented and reviewed. Risk is inevitable in introducing change. Principal has to be competent enough to add values in the components of change. Principal being the Transformer, has to keep pace with the latest developments, Researches Innovations and Practices in order to plan and implement the change.

Principal's ability to explore several alternatives, full involvement of one and all and seek cooperation of team members can further facilitate change management. Numerous challenges may have to be encountered in the implementation of change. These can be met by collective efforts, shared Vision, setting benchmarks and standards. Proactive role of Principal is very essential for high productivity and performance.

Change can be implemented with internal sources as people and resources

within. People and resources can be hired from elsewhere also. Incredible courage is required to introduce change. Well planned strategies, effective interpersonal communication, training, experience, self awareness and willingness are some of the essentials of change management. **Leader can succeed and survive only when the change yields desired results.**

The leader at the same time must also ensure that the change doesn't cause negative consequences in the long run.

Now the New Mantra is ' Transform or Perish'.

5.Team Building

Coming together is beginning

keeping together is progress

Working together is a success.

Team is a group of people working towards achieving a common goal. Team Building is a skill. It is one of the most significant attributes of Leadership. Principal has to form several teams for the smooth functioning of the Institution and assign them responsibilities. The team members cooperate and coordinate with each other and work in accordance with the instructions and guidance of the Principal.

The role of every Team Member in the accomplishment of tasks must be clearly defined. Unless the team members understand the task the positive results are difficult to achieve. Strong Leadership, effective Communication, timely feedback, motivation and team spirit contribute to the success of the team to a larger extent.

If you want to go fast go alone

If you want to go far, go together.

Alone I can say but together we can talk

Alone I can enjoy but together we can celebrate.

Alone I can smile but together we can laugh.

To achieve common goal interdependence, trust, mutual understanding, enthusiasm, zeal are necessary. *While forming teams Principal has to keep in mind their individual competencies, knowledge and skills*. The commitment and sense of accountability of team members bring them success.

Sometimes Teams can be ineffectiv, dysfunctional and disruptive. This may cause poor performance and results. In such a situation the Principal has to be vigilant. Individual suggestions of the members must be accorded due recognition and importance. Must avoid conflict.

The leader must encourage team participation as one entity ignoring their personal differences. Unity amongst the members is key to success. ' **United we stand, divided we fall'**. The team members must also be felicitated, due recognition be given and rewarded for their exemplary contributions.

6.Influencing

Leadership is about influencing the individuals and groups towards achieving goals. Principal is said to have influenced only when the team is willingly accepting the responsibility and change. In order to influence the the people Principal must follow democratic and participative approach. Good interpersonal relationship and effective communication are the two basic requirements of the process of influencing. Principal not only influences through his leadership qualities but also guides and directs.

Leader's ability to persuade the team to seek defined objectives is another important attribute in influencing the team. The competency and effectiveness play a dominant role in influencing and impacting. Role modeling, setting examples and Principal's initiatives certainly leave an everlasting effect. Principal has to be supportive and display humanity, conscience and positiveness in functioning. Should always be vying for growth and development.

Leader must lead from front but at the same time the leader must pave the way to others to lead. In Fact leadership is to create leaders not followers.

Prime Minister Narendra Modi has very rightly quoted that these days the Govts. and the organizations are trapped in A B C D.

- **A**void
- **B**ypass
- **C**onfuse
- **D**elay

There is a need to convert this acronym into R O A D ie:

- **R**esponsibility
- **O**wnership
- **A**ccountability
- **D**iscipline

This is very relevant to leadership also.

CHAPTER XI

Principal as a Trainer of Staff

The Principalbeing the Institutional Head is responsible for the Professional Development of the Faculty. Without a futuristic growth neither the faculty nor the Institution can survive in this era of cut throat competition. **Training is the most tested and trusted tool of Professional Development.**

Finest training facilities at Institution level will turn the faculty into skilled professionals and hone them into tough and tenacious jobs. The effective training enables the teachers to transfer their knowledge and skills to the classroom. **Training sharpens the shaw, opens mind, develops curiosity and instils an appetite for learning.**

Principal while inducting the new faculty must play a proactive role in the settlement and adjustment of them. They are totally unaware of the system and therefore, need to be adopted and guided. They should be welcomed as guests, should be respected, give them positive feedback, pay personal attention , listen patiently and invest some quality time in them. **These are some of the informal techniques of training. They will certainly learn out of all these.**

What is Training?

It **is a planned and systematic process to develop knowledge , skills and attitude of the people.** In the process of professional growth knowledge is a dominant component. **For the faculty knowledge refers to mastery of the subject taught, its scope, subject matter, latest developments, researches, experimentations** etc. Unless the teacher is abreast with all these developments, justice can not be done with Teaching Learning.

Skill is the ability to perform. Having good knowledge of a subject doesn't suffice the professional growth. **Teaching in fact is an art, a skill.** Even after possessing sound knowledge, some teachers are not able to teach because of lack of confidence, exposure or methodology.

Attitude is the way we think, act and behave. It is the most important determinant of one's Professional Growth. The Research reveals that most successful people in the world were and are at helm not because they were very intelligent, knowledgeable and skilful but because of their positive outlook towards self and others. **Attitude matters a lot towards Professional Development.**

Training is basically a Professional Development Program. Since the Principals and Teachers are into the Human Development Field, training becomes more important and relevant. Training encourages the faculty to acquire new knowledge and skills, builds their competence and confidence, makes them more valuable and responsible. **Through robust interventions and facilitations Principal can create several avenues for the growth and development of faculty.**

Training develops both scientific and social understandings. The teachers need to have a scientific outlook and social skills which in turn will filter downwards to the students. Training therefore, provides the most appropriate and reasonable platform for professional development. In a knowledge driven society one has to gather information and acquire knowledge as much as possible. Training brings out hidden talents, prepares the trainees to be efficient and effective and enables them to realise the goals of the organisation.

The Principal holds the pivotal position in the Institution and therefore, the professional growth of teachers becomes the primary concern of the Head.

Training is not a panacea for all ills. The trainer as well as the trainee have to be very honest while receiving and giving the training inputs. **In absence of interest, willingness and penchant for learning, any training will have no positive impact.**

Principal can initiate this endeavour either by:

Providing On the Job or Institutional based Training.

OR

Sponsoring them for Off the Job Training elsewhere.

Principal although is responsible for both above yet the Institutional Level Training is Principal's prime responsibility.

1.On the Job Training

It **is imparted at the workplace. Principal is the Key Resource Person and the Master Trainer** for On the Job Training. Principal's effectiveness and flair for training make such training a Real Learning Event. Some senior faculty members can also assist the Principal in training the newly inducted teachers.

Principal has several training methods at his disposal. The experience and expertise of the Principal, knowledge, confidence and exposure, personality traits, values, principles and attitude are the attributes that make a Principal the best On the Job Trainer.

The following tools and techniques are beneficial for Institutional based training.

.Motivation

If the employees are motivated at the time of their induction, they feel attached and affiliated to the system. Principal can arrange an introductory session for the newly appointed faculty. **Apprise them of the Vision, Mission, aims, objectives, organisational structure and their role and responsibilities.** The Principal must also tell them about themselves and the priorities. By this exercise they will be able to know each other. This can be organised in-group as well as individually. The newcomers should be motivated in such a style,tone and tenor **that they get a feel of having joined the right system.**

.Observation

Principal should be the keen observer of the overall behaviour of the staff. By simple observational technique the Principal can make them learn and grow. Principal can record the observations of teaching, behaviour, dress and address, dealings, sincerity, responsibility, discipline etc. and bring them to the notice of the concerned faculty members. Appropriate suggestions and guidance can be given to rectify and improve. **This can be a very simple and** useful way of training. But the Principal must not be very critical in observing and conveying the Observations.

Coaching

It **is one to one interaction between the Principal (Trainer) and the Teacher** (Trainee,) The Principal is a Coach who gives some tips, suggests some techniques and also gives specific instructions to learn and improve. The trainee becomes more attentive and hence learns better. **Principal can talk, discuss, suggest, listen and** motivate in this process.

.Group Exercise

On the Job training can also be conducted in groups. The Principal is the Chief Resource Person and can also involve some senior faculty members. In a group some activity or a problem can be discussed. It **is a kind of Simulation in which some artificial situation can be created to study the real situation.** Learning develops through discussions and experiences known as Experiential Learning.

.Counseling and Guidance.

Principal has also to play the role of a *Counsellor and a Guide.* It is one of the important methods of In House Training.

Counselling is expert assistance provided to the trainee. Although it is the job of the Professional in this area yet the Principal is also a Professional and an expert of Pedagogical concerns.

Guidance is the advice given by the seniors to the juniors. The purpose of both is to make them learn, improve, perform and grow. Both Counselling and Guidance can be arranged either individually or in groups.

Supervision and Inspection

Principal is not only the observer but also the supervisor of the faculty. **It is the prerogative as well as the duty and responsibility of the Principal to supervise the instructional process in the classes.** While inspecting and supervising, the Principal may come across a number of merits as well as the demerits of the teachers. Principal being an experienced and senior person has the ability to identify all the traits and qualities required for effective teaching and learning. The observations recorded in this process should be shared with the persons supervised in a very positive manner.

Mentoring

Mentoring is the process of sharing the personal experiences, knowledge and skills of a senior person with the juniors. **In this process the Principal becomes the Mentor for the teachers who are the mentees.** Principal thus is the Role Model for them and advises, guides and suggests them in accordance to his own experiences and makes them learn. **This is an influencing process, the Principal makes efforts to impress and influence by sharing, building good relationships, providing them opportunity to come forward with their views,** problems and give possible solutions.

Communication

Both verbal and non-verbal communication are very relevant and important tools of on the job training. Principal through his oratory skills, expressions, body language, eye contact, circulars, office orders, speeches can pass on information to the staff and students. These can be in the forms of instructions, suggestions , guidelines, orders and requests. Effective communication can therefore, be very useful and beneficial in imparting informal on the job training.

Staff Meetings

Conduct of timely staff meeting is an integral component of Institutional Development. It provides a platform to the Principal and staff to discuss the Academic and non-academic issues and to arrive at conclusion. Conduct of meeting, fixing agenda and initiating discussions should be very effective so that all are fully involved, attentive, participative and contributive. The doubts should also be cleared amicably. In such meetings where the participation is of entire staff and they are given liberty to contribute, many ideas flow in and flow out which is a Learning in itself. If *conducted in a befitting manner and cordial environment, staff meetigs can prove to be the best Learning Events.*

2. OFF THE JOB TRAINIG.

TO keep the the faculty abreast with the latesr trends and developments in the field of teaching learning the principal needs to sponsor them for off the job training. most commonly known training programs are....

Induction Training.

orientation courses.

Workshops.

symposiums

Seminars.

Conferences.

Advantages of Training..

Training whether On the Job or Off the Job is beneficial for both the trainee and the Institution.

Advantages of the Trainee...

1.Development of knowledge, skills and attitude.

2.Enhances Personal and Professional Effectiveness.

3.Builds Competence and Capacity.

4.Develops Learning Habits.

Advantages of the Institution...

1.Accomplishment of Vision and Mission.

2.YieldsQuality Results.

3.Higher Efficiency and Productivity.

4.Optimum utilization of Resources.

5.Human Resource Development.

CHAPTER XII

Institutional Planning

Planning is of paramount importance to any organisation. In absence of systematic planning and its effective implementation Institutional objectives can not be realised.

Institutional Planning is a milestone in the journey of educational developments. It is a systematic need based plan prepared in advance by the Institution for its overall development i.e. academic, non-academic, infrastructural and human resources.

It is a comprehensive plan for the development and growth.

In the process of institutional planning all the functionaries and beneficiaries are actively involved and their wholehearted cooperation and support is sought. The primary objective is Institutional reforms, Improvements and Developments. Innovative and creative potentials of human resources are fully utilised. A systematic, informative and innovative planning can create quality based excellent, productive, progressive and perfect Institution.

Objectives

The first and foremost objective is to improve the overall functioning of the Institution. It reminds and directs the management of its responsibilities towards Institutional Development. The vision and mission of the Institution must be realised through the planned strategies. It aims at

Optimum utilisation of available resources. Ensures least wastage.

It provides opportunity to the teachers and taught to share their views and opinions and thus contribute significantly.

Ensures quality education through quality teaching learning strategies. The planning aims at excellence in scholastic and co scholastic spheres.

Shifting emphasis from teacher's centred education to learner centred education. Planning is formulated in such a way that the Institution becomes a Learning Organization in real sense. **The plan inspires meaningful Learning beyond prescribed syllabus and beyond the classroom.**

Setting Result Oriented Strategies, following them in letter and spirit. **Valiant efforts are made to accomplish the planned objectives.**

Undertakes several developmental **programmes for professional growth.** Spelling out the priorities and strategies to yield good results.

Making every drive in the plan an experience and setting the examples.

Nature and characteristics of Institutional Planning..

It **is comprehensive and Inclusive. Developmental plan is for overall growth** and involves all stakeholders. It is a cooperated and coordinated venture of the Institution.

Institutional Planning is for building the image of the Institution so that it is par excellence and known for its name and fame in the society.

Human, physical and financial resources are put to their fullest utilisation and efforts are made to draw maximum out of them. If any of the resources remain unutilized or underutilised, the planning is said to have failed.

It focuses both on improvement and development. Improvement is expected to be brought by the Principal, faculty and students. Development is the responsibility of all stakeholders including the management, authority, govt. and the community.

Planning is **for both long and short terms. Targets beyond the capacity and capability are not fixed. These should be achievable.**

Pursuit of Excellence in every field is ensured. Aims at Perfection in every affair of the Institution so that it becomes a brand apart. Its competitor is itself. To excel in every sphere specific strategies are planned after having thought provoking sessions with all concerned.

Recommendations and suggestions in the State and National Education Policies are also duly considered while formulating the plan. These policies provide guidance to formulate the plan.

Planning is not rigid, a flexible plan provides better opportunities for overall growth and development. The plan can be revised and reviewed if need be.

Scope of Institutional Planning.

The scope is vast and varied as it is not confined to any specific area of the Institution but to the entire gamut of the Institution. The scope can be discussed as under..

Instructional Improvement

1. Quality Instructional process is the most essential parameter of any Educational Institution. Development of quality teaching learning materials, interactive and innovative practices, staff development programs, creation of a suitable and congenial learning environment are the integral components of the Institutional Planning.

2. Timetable, allotment of duties and responsibilities, formation of subject committees, schedules of examination, coverage of syllabus, revision strategies, remedial teaching, quality result strategies are some of the pedagogical concerns given due importance in the planning.

3. Strengthening the support system..

Institutional planning is meant for the development of the whole plant. Therefore, support system needs to be strengthened to achieve the fixed targets.

Good infrastructure, labs, library, play fields, technology, audio visual aids, basic amenities provide big support to the Institutional Development and therefore, very significant areas of the planning.

4 Curricular and co-curricular Activities..

These activities lay the foundation of excellence. Gone are the days of Academic Excellence when the marks and merits played a dominant role. **The present and future belongs toExcellence everywhere.** Therefore, these activities need to be planned and organised meticulously for wholesome development of the learners. **Academic and Activities calendars are** prepared after giving serious thoughts by the planners so that the same are organised timely and effectively.

5. Staff Development

The areas planned above can not show any symbols of Development unless the faculty is enriched and equipped with necessary tools, techniques, knowledge and skills from time to time. Therefore, training both on the job and off the job, workshops, induction, orientation, seminars etc are essential for professional growth.

6 .Career counselling and Guidance..

Inthis era of competition, the students need to be counselled and guided about their future endeavours. Due importance is accorded to these activities in Institutional Planning.

7. Alumni Cell.

Alumni play a very positive role in Institutional Development. If tapped effectively, Alumni can prove to be an important asset to the Institution. Therefore, Alumni Meet, their contributions, their contacts and the suggestions need due consideration. Since the students who passed out may have settled in various professions, their experiences and suggestions will be valuable for the growth of the Institution.

Essentials of good Institutional Planning

It must be continuous and creative.

It should be time bound, the targets fixed must be realised within the stipulated time.

It must be motivating so that it is effectively implemented and executed.

It must have an inbuilt controlling system.

Planning process in depth must be communicated and explained to the lowest level of functionaries.

People are the essence of planning, their contributions, cooperation and coordination are significant factors in the success of planning.

Components of Institutional Planning

It consists of the following...

1.The Objectives of the Institution to be achieved.

2.Various Policies and Procedures of the Institution.

3.Rules and Regulations.

4.Budgetary Provisions.

5.Strategies to be adopted to achieve the targets fixed.

Advantages of good planning

Prepares the Institution to meet the challenges and face competition with others

It is cost effective and minimises cost.

Limitations of Planning...

1.Effective Implementation is the main hindrance in the success of Planning. Even if the planning is meticulously designed with all its essentials, any lapse in implementation will prove to be hazardous.

2.Risk is the biggest challenge. Good *Planning of course minimises the risk but can not eliminate it.*

3.Some of the Internal and External variables can be beyond the control of the Planners.

4.If the information gathered is not authentic and reliable, the planning may not succeed.

Principal being the administrative head and main executor, should be a driving force behind the effective implementation and success of the planning.

CHAPTER XIII

Communication

In this era of Globalisation communication is very crucial. May it be administration, management or Leadership, communication plays a pivotal role. Effective communication builds good relations, eradicates misunderstandings and promotes mutual trust. In educational Institutions where the best platforms are provided for wholesome development and the future of the nation is prepared, it is more important.

The objectives, policies, procedures and all the affairs of the Institution can be explained and understood only through the process of effective communication. Principal , being the head of the Institution, is responsible for communicating all these to the stakeholders. If not communicated clearly the same can neither be understood nor comprehended.

Communication is a meaningful interaction between those who speak or listen, read or write. The spirit of communication lies in fostering intelligible dialogue between two parties. It is the transmission of information and knowledge from one mind to another or to a group of people.

Communication is not just an exchange of words but an expression of a deeper understanding of one another. Effective communication is so long as the other person is able to understand. Communication is more than messaging, it is over and above talking, speaking and listening.

Personal Interactions are the most important medium of Communication. There is no replacement for these tools. Hence the Principal of the Institution must accord top priority to this medium. This is the best way to communicate, to make them learn and to understand. Such communication can make phenomenal strides in quality teaching learning and overall functioning of the Institution.

Academic Institutions are Teaching Intensive. Failure of communication at any level is likely to result in various problems pertaining to discipline, quality, values, work environment etc. Therefore, the Principal must strengthen the communication mechanism and hone his communication skills time and again.

Principles of Good Communication

1. The information to be conveyed **should be brief.** Very lengthy conversation is neither understood nor it conveyed any meaning.

2. It **should be Natural.** Reality should reflect in the words of the Person who is communicating. Good communication must be clear.

3. **communication should** be **simple.** Complicated speeches, lectures, letters, drafts, interactions become difficult to comprehend.

4. It **should be Impressive.** Whatever is communicated in words or letters should impress and influence the people being involved.

5. **Adequacy is another feature of** good communication. Whatever is communicated should be sufficient and complete to be understood.

6. **Drawing attention of recipients is** an integral feature of good communication. If the recipients do not pay any attention to the communicator and the information communicated, communication is said to be ineffective.

7 .**Communication has to be vivid and consistent..**

Types of Communication..

Verbal/ oral communication...

Words are very important in communicating ideas or sending messages.

Non-verbal Communication. .

Transmitting messages without words or letters. Many things can very effectively be conveyed through Body Languages, facial expressions, eye contacts, gestures and postures. In an Educational Institution this type of communication is very common and also useful.

Formal and Informal Communication..

Formal Communication is in official terms ie to communicate through letters, circulars, memos, official orders. It follows some prescribed rules and procedures. **Informal Communication on the other hand is friendly interactions, chats, talks etc.** Such communication does not follow any strict code but has to be sobre and unobjectionable. It is normal and day to day communication.

Horizontal Communication..

This communication is **from work groups to their managers.** A candid exchange of ideas takes place in such communication. This is straight interaction with each other, makes them easily available and keep the ball rolling. By this medium even tough jobs become easy to handle.

Vertical Communication

This is from the superiors to the subordinates. It can be upward as well as downward ie from the Principal to the staff and students and vice versa

Advantages of Communication

The **Principal** is supposed to be the best communicator in the Institution. The main function of the Principal is Communication. *All the times the Principal is communicating only.* Passing the information, instructions, orders, conducting meetings, interactions with teachers, students parents and other stakeholders is all communication. Therefore, the Principal must be an effective and influential communicator so that he/she is able to convince them. **Communication skills assist the Principal as under...**

Good relationships can be cultivated by honing our communication skills. This is the best way to develop healthy relations. Good relations can be developed with superiors, colleagues and subordinates by effective communication.

Helps in **managing both the Hard as well as the Soft sides** of the job.

Clear, *complete and consistent messages can be effectively delivered.*

Communication is the best medium to solve problems. Most of the problems crop up not on account of '*What We Say but How We*

Say.'

Generous and courteous communication is the best introduction. Greater the Courtesy, Stronger is the relationship.

It facilitates all managerial functions of planning, organising, directing, controlling and evaluating. In this complexity of time good administration and management is impossible without effective communication.

Communication is very essential for building Institutional Image. Image is dependent on effective interpersonal communication to a much larger extent.

Communication enhances both productivity and proficiency. In Academic Institutions Quality Results can be achieved with the help of frequent, relevant and effective communication among all stakeholders.

Barriers of Communication..

Sometimes communication does not serve the purpose may be because it is not effective, meaningful and clear. All these adversely affect the process of communication and thus cause a breakdown.

A. Mechanical Barriers..

These barriers are caused due to the casual approach of both the communicator and the recipients. These may also occur because of delay and distance.

B. Organizational Barriers..

Process of communication may also be hampered due to the policies, rules, regulations of the organisation. It happens when the employees are not having clear understanding of all these or the same were not effectively communicated.

How the communication is Received, Perceived and Comprehended matters a lot.

C. Personal Barriers...

Employees dissatisfaction, lack of incentives, poor promotional avenues and attitude of superiors also deter the communication process. The employees may not respond to the comminiques seriously due to these adverse factors.

Causes of Barriers..

Poor Timing

Sometimes communication is not on time and therefore, not properly interpreted.

Inappropriate Channels

The communication channels must be appropriate. The communicator has to ascertain the suitability of the channel or the medium of communication. **Failing which communication will not be received and perceived properly.**

Language

If the language of communication is not understood, it will not convey any sense and will cause a barrier in the process.

Difference in perceptions and emotions

Mismatch between the perceptions and emotions of the sender and receiver also cause hindrance. The sender wants to convey something, the receivers percieves something else.

Poor and Casual Listening

This is perhaps the most common cause of barriers. When the information passed on orally is not given a patient listening and not taken seriously, the communication is not successful.

Overloaded Information

When the information is hotch potch, mixed up and not clear, the recipients will be in confusion status and information remains unconveyed.

Process of Communication

Communication is a continuous process. It is always two ways. Communication takes place only when we have something to express. Therefore, the ideas emerge in the mind of the communicator. These are communicated through a medium which must be understood and responded to by the communicatee.

The process of communication involves the following:

Message

The ideas formed in the mind of the communicator become messsge.It is the first and foremost. It is the message/es to be transmitted from one person to another or teams/groups. Messages can be oral, written, verbal or non-verbal.

Sender

Sender is the source of messages. Sender has to decide the text, medium,and language of the message.

Encoding

It is to give proper form to the message so that it becomes meaningful. The sender may translate his thoughts into a language of choice or may use codes and symbols.

Medium

The sender chooses the language in which the message is to be communicated. The language should be convenient for both the sender and recipients.

Recipient/Communicate

The receiver of the message who receives, perceives and comprehends the message.

Decoding

The recipient interprets the message. Tries to understand the meaning and purpose of the message.

Feedback

It is the reaction, response or reply of the recipient. It can be verbal as well as nonverbal.

Elements of Communication

Preparation of Message

It can be in the form of facts, ideas, complaints, notices, orders etc.

Sending Message by a medium.

Receiving a message by the receiver.

Channelizing the message.

Symbolising the message or encoding.

Characteristics of good Communication

It should be relevant and in accordance with the objectives.

It is complete, clear, explanatory and concise.

Effective subject matter and language.

Good communication is effective, impressive, emotional, polite and human.

Objectives of Communication

Passing Information and Instructions
Sharing information.
Gathering feedback.
Strengthening control.
Solving problems.
Decision making.
Facilitating change.
Importance of Communication
It is necessary for Planning.
Basis of cooperation and coordination.
Effective Leadership. Enhances Managerial and Leadership Skills.
Basis of Decision meaning and Action taking.
Morale boosting and Motivation.
Smooth Functioning of the Institution.
Growth and Development.

Therefore, the most important tool with the Principal is Communication which is very useful in informing, enquiring, influencing, motivating, educating, convincing, consoling, clarifying and many others.

CHAPTER XIV

Conduct of Effective Meetings

The Principal of the Institution has to remain in constant touch with the staff and students. In order to establish this relation, Meetings are the most appropriate instruments. Such meetings can be formal as well as informal. But both will involve communication and the success of the meeting will be determined by the quality, seriousness and effectiveness of the meeting.

The Principal being the Top Line Manager is responsible for planning and conducting meetings from time to time to suggest, instruct, direct control and guide the staff, students, parents and others.

Techniques of conducting meetings

Conducting meetings is not a simple task. It is rather a thoughtful exercise. It needs thorough planning and preparation. The leader has to keep several things in mind and proceed further accordingly. The following techniques are are involved in the conduct of meeting...

Planning..

It is the most significant component of any meeting. The success and effectiveness of a meeting is largely dependent on its planning. The conductor has to decide the Agenda on the basis of the feedback gathered and own observations, opinions and suggestions. Time, place, duration are important parts of Planning.

Agenda...

This is the list of issues to be discussed or to be undertaken in the meeting. It is prepared in such a manner that all important and relevant issues are included and time is not wasted on unnecessary and irrelevant issues. The objective of the Agenda is to inform the participants in advance about the subject matter to be discussed. The agenda of Formal Meetings is generally circulated and suggestions are invited so that the participants are prepared and they take interest in the deliberations.

Meetings can be effective and informative only when the agenda is followed. Deviation from the agenda hampers the entire exercise and the whole purpose is defeated. This will not only make the meeting a success but also develop curiosity and interest for future meetings as well.

Participation...

Without active participation of one and all the meetings will not yield any results. Inviting participation is in fact a skill. The main person to plan and conduct the meeting must be competent enough to initiate participation by his inspirational and motivational styles. The participants must be encouraged to come forward with their viewpoints.

The Principal must encourage participation from those who talk too little and control those who talk too much. The dominance of the talkative should be discouraged and the introverted employees should be encouraged to speak and participate.

Effective participation will pave the way to fruitful Discussions. The purpose is served only when the issue is discussed at length with its pros and cons.

Cooperation and coordination...

Meeting needs a very cordial and congenial environment. In absence of a favourable environment meetings can not be effective and useful. The Principal has to seek cooperation from all and coordinate with them accordingly.

Summarizing...

After having discussed the agenda points the Principal has to conclude. While concluding the Principal has to make sure that all points have figured and discussed. The summary of the meeting reminds the participants of the points discussed.

This is the process of winding up the meeting. The Principal must ask the participant about any other issue to be discussed or their suggestions. This will enable them to share their views which have not been included in the Agenda.

Code of Conduct..

Proper decorum is to be maintained during the meeting. Any hot arguments, indiscipline, need to be controlled efficiently. Principal has to establish eye contact with all the attendees in order to draw their attention and keep them on the track.

Time schedule fixed for the meeting is another important component. The Principal has to ensure that the participants turn on time, there are no absentees, meeting commences on time and concludes timely. There should be no wastage of time.

Minutes of the Meeting...

All formal meetings must be followed by proper minutes. **Minutes are the official records of the proceedings and the decisions taken in the meeting.** This is the brief written account of the meeting. There is a person in charge to take up this assignment, could be staff secretary or any other suitable person selected by the principal. He/she will note down all the points discussed, decisions taken and suggestions given. The minutes must be written in appropriate language which can be understood by all.

There are several reasons for writing the minutes ....

This provides a basis for the follow up.

Minutes are the evidences of the attendees coming together, discussions, interactions, decisions and suggestions.

These are the references for the people who were unable to attend due to one or the other reasons. A quick look at the minutes will apprise them of the highlights of the meeting.

Minutes remind the participants of their **assurances and promises made** for the Institutional Development.

Writing the minutes is a thoughtful exercise. The composer has to keep all deliberations in mind and ascertain nothing is left. He/she has to be amply clear of the objective. Very difficult language should be avoided.

The minutes must be circulated among all the concerned and get signed by them.

Types of Meetings..

Basically meetings are of two types..

Informal Meetings...

These are the routine meetings. Principal has to interact with staff and students on a variety of issues in day to day affairs. Such meetings have no designed agenda, time and place. Sometimes Informal meetings prove to be very useful as the interactions and discussions take place cordially. In educational Institutions where the staff and students are in constant touch with each other, informal meetings are more important.

Formal Meetings..

These are the official meetings having an agenda, time, place and participants. These can be fortnightly or monthly. All proceedings of such meetings are recorded.

Besides, **there are some Mini Meetings** also.

These can be both formal as well as Informal. For smooth functioning the Principal forms various committees and Clubs. These committees and clubs assist the Principal and the faculty to share some of their work loads and thus play a vital role in Institutional Growth. This paves way to decentralization of authority which is an important component of a Democratic System.

Meetings of these committees are conducted from time to time. Such committees are for both Scholastic as well as co-Scholastic spheres.Some of these are mentioned below..

Subject Committees...

These are formed for discussing and introducing latest inventions and innovations in the subject. The Departmental Heads are the incharges of the committees of their respective subjects.

Timetable Committee..

This committee frames the Timetable of the Institution. The incharge is some senior faculty member. The committee allots periods and also makes alternative arrangements

Examination Committee..

The responsibility of the conduct of examination is assigned to this committee. The committee gets the question papers set, prepares examination schedules, arranges for evaluation and consolidates results.

Discipline Committee.

Discipline lays the foundation of success of any Institution in general and Educational Institution in particular.. In every Institution there is a Discipline Committee which assists the Principal in maintaining proper discipline. The principal nominates strict disciplinarians in this committee. The Committee conducts routine meetings and meets whenever need be.

CCA Committee...

Co Curricular Activities are very essential not only to keep the students gainfully busy but also for their wholesome development. The teachers are given responsibilities in this committee on the basis of their interest and willingness.

Gender Harassment Committee..

In every Institution some cases of gender harassment occur. These problems adversely affect the smooth functioning of the Institution. There is an Institution level committee to solve such matters amicably.

Parent Teacher Association.

Parents are the most important stakeholders in every Institution. Their suggestions and feedback are always valuable in the progress of the Institution. There is a PTA in every Institution. Meetings are conducted from time to time.

Sports Committee...

Sports are the integral components of the Institution. These help in image building as well as physical development of the students. The Sports Committee organises various sports activities and suggests ways and means for the promotion of sports.

Science Club.

The club consists of some science teachers and students.The main function of Science Club is to develop scientific temperament and organize Scientific Activities as exhibition, debates, quiz on science topics, photography etc.

Literary Club.

The Literary Club organises various literary activities in which maximum participation of students is encouraged. Dramatics, declamation, debates, extempore speeches are some of the activities undertaken by the club. Meeting of club members is organised from time to time.

Alumni Meets..

Alumni Association is formed in every Institution. Both former and ex-students contribute significantly to the Institutional Development. These students always like to give back something to their Alma Mater. It may be in the form of some Physical Asset, suggestions, Guidance etc. Alumni meets should be organised in a befitting manner.

The Mentor of above Committees and Clubs is the Principal. Therefore, the presence of the Principal is obligatory. Owing to the busy schedule Principal may not be able to attend the meeting of every committee but the feedback of the outcome of the meeting must be gathered.

Some DOs and Don'ts of Perfect Meeting..

Perfection is something we all strive for in our professional personal, social and professional lives.

DOs...

Plan in advance and Be Prepared for the meeting.

Manage the Time and avoid wastage.

Exercise Command and control when things go out of hand.

Proper eye contact and appropriate body language are essential.

Invite participation and involve all.

Initiate fruitful discussions.

Present the subject matter effectively.

Add humour in expression.

Evaluate the meeting.

Don'ts..

The attendees should not be discouraged to come forward.

Don't try to dominate, deviate, divide and disagree.

Avoid arguments and confrontation.

Avoid repetition.

According to Satya Nadella, the IT wizard, three rule methods for better meetings are...

Listen more, Talk less and be decisive when time comes.

CHAPTER XV

Building A Learning Organization

'**Come to Learn and Go to Serve**' is often seen written at the front gate of most Educational Institutions. In Fact the Academic Institutions are meant for Learning. A good teacher is not one whose teaching is excellent but one who makes the students learn.

Learning is defined as an ability to acquire knowledge and set of skills . It is a process of a desirable modification in behaviour.

Organization consists of people serving a system to achieve a common objective.

Learning Organization provides opportunities to learn, develop and transform. In Such organizations People have tremendous scope to acquire knowledge, hone their skills, and develop a positive attitude. They transform themselves and are able to transfer the learning. Learning is a lifelong process and **Learning Organization facilitates learning and initiates learning to learn and grow.**

Learning Organisation has its own mechanism for continual growth of its employees, capacity building and they are continuously learning to learn. It provides ample opportunities to enhance both individual and collective learning.

As the emphasis has now shifted to Learning from Teaching, every Institution strives hard to become a Learning Organization where not only the students learn at an alarming rate bur the teachers also continuously make good efforts to update themselves with latest trends, innovations, researches and experimentations. They are always learners and transfer their learning to the students.

Why Learning Organization?.

There is tuff competition everywhere. We can not survive unless we are fully prepared to meet the challenges. This can happen only when we are continuous learners and updating ourselves.

It is not only the **competition but the rapid changes in processes, procedures, policies, technology and other fields**. To adapt the change we need to learn and grow.

Accomplishment of the Vision and Mission is not possible unless we are learning. Our Learning will enhance if the organization we are serving has the scope to learn.

Coping with Rapid and Unexpected Changes.

Changes are now universal. In almost every Fields changes are taking place not only rapidly but frequently also. Academic Institutions are also not unaffected. We have to introduce these changes to survive and grow. **Changes in processes, procedures, policies, methods, technology etc.are to be adapted and adopted.** The Learning Organization can not only manage but effectively implement these changes.

Facing the Competition..

Our existence is possible only when we are able to compete. Our competition is with others as well as with self. We need to set standards and benchmarks to compete with others and **'Doing Better Than Before'** to compete with ourselves. Continuous Learning is necessary to meet the challenges of competition. The Learning Organization builds competitive spirit and inspires the employees to face competition.

Personal and Professional Development..

Growth and Development are two basic requirements of every organization. The organizational growth is directly dependent on the effectiveness of its employees. If the employees are serious about their growth, they make good efforts to acquire knowledge and develop skills, their personal as well as professional effectiveness will also improve.The learning Organization can only provide the opportunities to grow.

Free exchange and flow of Information..

This is the age of Information. A variety of information needs to be gathered in order to learn and grow. Information is the biggest source of Knowledge. Fortunately there are several sources of Information available. Learning Organization creates good avenues for information acquisition, its management and sharing.

Total Quality Management..

Quality is perhaps the most dominating concept in personal and professional domains. Quality concept initially took place in Industry but now it is required everywhere. All educational initiatives of both public and private sectors focus on Quality. *Every Academic and Professional Institution aims at providing Quality Education, encourages quality teaching learning practices and leaves no stone unturned to produce Quality Results.* Therefore, quality is to be managed efficiently and effectively. A Learning Organization provides the best platform to achieve quality in every sphere.

Creating a climate of openness and Trust..

Forward looking approach, open mindedness and Trust Building are the essentials of self as well as the Institutional growth. The learning Organization encourages and enables the people to develop ideas, speak and spell them out and challenge the actions.

How do people learn?

There are several Learning Styles but most common of them are..

Learning by Being Told.

Learning By Doing.

Learning by Trial and Error.

Learning by Imitation.

Learning by experience.

All have their own pace of Learning snd therefore, follow the styles accordingly.

Pillars of learning...

Dellor's Commission has suggested the following four pillars which also define the purpose of Learning..

Learning to Know.

Learning to Do.

Learning to Be.

Learning to Live Together.

Learning to Learn was further added.

Our former President Dr. APJ Kalam added..

Learning to Grow and Learning to Survive.

The **purpose of life is also to LIVE, LOVE and LEARN.**

Building A Learning Organization..

It is neither a simple nor a short term process. It requires serious and sincere efforts by one and all. **Principal being the Front Line Manager, is the pace setter in this process.** The commitments and initiatives of the Principal, his acumenship, managerial and leadership qualities will support him in creating an environment for building a Learning Organization. Middle and bottom line workers need to be valued and utmost efforts to build their competence and confidence are required.

The following management processes need to be adopted to build a Learning Organization.

Strategic Planning..

Planning is the first and foremost process in creating a Learning Organisation. Principal has to think **Out Of Box,** plan suitable and appropriate strategies, and implement them effectively. The plans should be well thought and goal oriented.

Management of Information and Knowledge.

This is the age of Information.The biggest source of Knowledge is Information. Variety of Information is available through various sources. Every Institution has to develop its own **MIS(Management of Information System) Information** can become the greatest Resource if collected timely, it is relevant, analysed and used appropriately. Learning Organization converts the Information into Learning.

Capacity Building...

EveryInstitution must provide adequate opportunities to its employees to enhance their capacity and grow. Capability is the main force behind the success of every Organization. The Learning Organization is built by competent and capable people. Therefore, Capacity Building Programs are very necessary. These programs can be Institution based as well as elsewhere. The capacity can be built by effective training programs, constant dialogues with fellow workers and by reskilling and upskilling them.

Experiential Learning..

Experience is the best teacher. We learn from our own experiences as well of others. Experiential Learning is the best learning.Whatever we learn from each other, the experiences in training programs, class room experiences, experiences of gatherings, meetings collectively become Experiential Learning. Building a Learning Organization is an emergent need to fully utilize experiential Learning.

Transfer of Learning.

It has been often experienced that people learn a lot through various sources but unfortunately the same is not transferred to the real beneficiaries. For example, whatever knowledge is gained and skills developed while attending professional development courses, the teachers are not able to transfer the same to the students in the classroom owing to one or the other reasons. There is tremendous scope of Transfer of Learning in Learning Organization.

Learning Environment..

In absence of a congenial Learning Culture, no Institution can become a Learning Organization. Even after having a team of competent people and all resources, lack of a suitable environment will not serve the purpose of Building a Learning Organization.

It is the Learning Environment which provides ample opportunities to learn.

Performance Management..

' **Perform or Perish' is the Management Mantra.** How is the performance of the people, what are their potentials, how to tap the potentials, performance indicators and parameters, performance analysis, measurement, ways and means to enhance performance are some of the areas of Performance Management. If managed effectively, people willingly learn and a Learning Institution is built.

Rewards and Recognitions ..

The appreciation of employees for their accomplishments, giving due recognition to their performance, rewarding and awarding them are the morale boosting techniques, they feel motivated and learn more and more in order to bring further laurels. When the employees have a learning attitude and are interested to continue to the best of their capabilities, the Institution automatically becomes a Learning Organization.

Empowering the Employees..

Effective Leaders always empower the fellow workers to enable them to perform better. Giving autonomy to express their views, ideas, sharing experiences and taking initiatives enhances their motivation level, confidence and commitment. The **empowered work force can produce unparalleled and unmatchable results and thus are supportive to building a Learning Organization.**

Features of Learning Organization..

From the above description of Learning Organization We can now draw its salient features..

Existence of *Learning Environment is* the foremost among all.

People are constant learners. They keep on acquiring new knowledge and develop abilities.

The learning styles, tools and techniques can be different but the **objective is the same i.e. transformation.**

Enhancement in **competitive zeal and team spirit.**

Builds trust, competence, confidence and commitment.

Enables the people to cope with **challenges and uncertainties.**

Job satisfaction, happiness factor and performance are on the higher side.

Principal is the key person in the system. Therefore, the sole responsibility to build Learning Organisation lies with him. But at the same time the team can not skip. the responsibilities. Building lO is a coordinated effort. All stakeholders must contribute with accordance to their latent potentials and capabilities. If so, the Institution is bound to become a **Prodigious Center of Learning.**

Learning Organization ultimately leads the team to Dedication, Motivation, Commitment, Achievement and finally yo excellence.

CHAPTER XVI

Problem Solving

One of the finest attributes of Leadership is Problem Solving. It is in fact a skill and ability. No system is without problems. Problems occur everywhere, the magnitude may be different. Educational Institutions are also not spared of Problems. The significance of Problem Solving becomes a matter of serious concern because of its Character and Nation Building Roles.

What is a Problem?

Any difficult situation to handle or manage becomes a problem. It can be an event, a situation or an individual. Any trouble that occurs in the system, is not curbed or controlled timely takes the form of a problem.There can be s problematic situation as well as a problematic person.If not handled properly, can cause a big harm to the Institution. The problem may take form of a Conflict or Crisis.

The **Educational Institutions are also not free from problems.** Principal has to come across a number of problems. Most of them are pertaining to Indiscipline.

Causes of Problems...

Absence of Cordial and CongenialEnvironment...

Sometimes the Environment in the Institution is not favourable.May be the work culture is missing, there is no coordination amongst the employees, there is leg pulling or the Head is not supportive. Owing to all this many problems take place in the system.

Ineffective Teaching Learning Practices..

Any Educational Institution earns name and fame due to its Quality Education and Effective Teaching Learning practices. Ineffective transactional methodology, poor learning, non-attentive and non-participatory Classes cause many problems.

Indiscipline...

Indiscipline among staff and students is the most dominating cause of problems. It can be due to violation of instructions, orders and the prescribed code of conduct. Both the students and staff can indulge in indiscipline.

Inadequate Support System.

Problems may also occur due to lack of physical facilities, basic amenities, insufficient infrastructure, library, labs, play fields etc. Inadequacy of all this adversely affects the functioning and keeps students and staff busy in undesirable activities. They are not gainfully busy and thus indulge in one or the other act of indiscipline.

No Suitable Complaint Mechanism..

The Principal, Heads of Dept. Incharges keep on receiving the complaints from the students, parents, teachers, authority and Community. Sometimes a serious view of these complaints is not taken, or the concerned persons take them casually, the complaint becomes the problem. Even a minor problem if not handled timely and amicably, the same becomes a major one and difficult to overcome.

Attitudes and Behaviours...

Negative thinking and undesirable behavioural patterns also cause several problems. It may be on the Part of Principal, faculty or students. Not taking things positively, misbehaving and disliking causes disturbances and gives rise to individual as well as the Institutional problems.. **Egoistic and erratic behavior leads to negativity.**

Misunderstandings..

Owing to poor Interpersonal relationships, a lot of misunderstandings are created. This may happen because of communication gap or absence of interaction or dialogue from time to time. When we don't understand each other nor make efforts to understand and to be understood, several problems crop up.

Safety and Security..

When the staff and students don't feel safe and secure in the Institution, proper security measures are not adopted, problems are bound to occur. Sometimes such problems take a serious shape and prove to be hazardous. Safety Audit is as important as accounts audit.

Improper Feedback Mechanism..

Feedback is gathering information about overall functioning of the Institution. The students, parents, teachers and other stakeholders are the sources of feedback. Feedback is received as well as given. Positive feedback strengthens the functioning whereas negative feedback is the matter of concern. If the feedback mechanism is not effective, the problems can not be identified and these remain problems and may also lead to several other problems.

In a nutshell various problems of the Institution can be summarized as...

Academic..

These problems may arise due to ineffective teaching, poor academic standard, unsatisfactory results, insufficient infrastructure and amenities, poor learning habits, non- attentive and non-participatory class etc.

Administrative..

Indiscipline amongst staff and students, non-compliance of instructions, arguments, fights, quarrels, clashes, gender issues, ragging, unfair decisions and biased actions cause a number of problems.

.Managerial ..

Many problems take place because of mis-handling, misunderstandings, communication gaps and poor intet-, personal relations.

Environmental.

Varied backgrounds of staff and students, absence of work culture, criticisms, ego clashes, leg pulling are also responsible for generating certain problems.. Fear mongering and threats disrupt the functioning of the Institution and cause problems for the Administration.

Attitudinal..

Negative thinking, misbehaviour, inappropriate body language, objectionable tone and tenor, harsh language also cause several problems.

Problem Solving..

Solving problems is not everybody's cup of tea. It is in fact a Leadership Quality. Problem Solving is a skill. Only efficient and effective leaders can solve problems amicably. Problems can be simple and complex. Simple problems may have immediate solutions but complicated problems need in depth analysis.

Problem solving is a process. Several steps are involved in this process. In the Institution it is the responsibility of the Principal to provide possible solutions to every problem. **The following steps, if adopted systematically, can assist the Principal in Problem Solving.**

Identifying and defining the Nature of the Problem..

As soon as the problem comes before the Principal, its nature, source and its gravity must be identified and defined. Without understanding the nature of Problem solution can not emerge. Whether the problem is simple or complex, from where it has occurred, what is the cause are some of the decisions taken.

Examining the Facts.

The factual status must also be examined. Principal has to make it sure that the problem really exists or not. Fact finding tactics need to be adopted. Feedback gathered in this regard will be of much importance. If the facts behind the problems are not examined, time will be wasted unnecessarily.

Root Cause Analysis.

After having known the problem and the factual position, the Principal has to find the root cause of the problem. One problem may have occurred due to several reasons but the root cause will be one. Forinstens if indiscipline is the Root Cause of a problem, systematic and schematic process needs to be undertaken to curb indiscipline. There may be some other causes as well, but having known the root cause, others will automatically disappear.

Root Cause Analysis is a thought provoking exercise for which a lot of Critical Thinking is required.. The Cause of Problem is analysed in detail, consultations are held, conclusions are drawn and possible solutions are found.

Considering the Alternatives...

A problem can be solved in different ways. An effective Principal will choose the best alternative. The pros and cons of the alternative chosen must thoroughly be examined before implementing the same. In case the alternative considered doesn't seem to be appropriate, another alternative should be applied

Involving All..

Problem Solving should be a democratic process. If not handled efficiently, desired results may not be yielded. It is better to include others so that it becomes an inclusive process. The result of Inclusion will be better because it will *be based on Shared Vision.* If others are involved, consulted and dialogues are held, There can be good number of solutions. The best one can be applied.

Determining the Course of Action..

Solution of any problem requires an action to be taken. The action must be in accordance with the gravity of the problem.It should be fair and without any biases. The Principal has therefore, be very careful while determining the course of Action.

Time Management..

Time is an important component in Problem Solving. Any problem that occurs in the Institution must be resolved timely. In case a problem remains for longer time, even a simple problem may take the form of a serious one. If timely action is taken solution becomes easier.

Implementation of action for solution..

Once the action to resolve the problem is decided, it should immediately be implemented. Any delay in Implementation may further lead to more problems and intensity may also increase.

Evaluation...

The action towards the solution needs to be evaluated from time to time. The solution sometimes may not work or may not have ever lasting impact. Therefore, the Principal has to evaluate in order to assess the failures. The remedial measures are possible only when the evaluation is done.

Utmost efforts need to be made to solve the problem at Institution level but Sometimes the Problem is so grave that the solution is not possible locally. At this stage some external intervention is also required. The assistance of some experts of the issue is sought to solve the problem. In such a situation the following procedures are adopted...

Arbitration..

It is Third-party Dispute Settlement. The Arbitrator is a legal expert but the problem is solved out of the Court. The negotiations are held between the disputing parties. The concerned parties are apprised of the legal formalities and complications. Therefore, the **Arbitrator suggests for Out of the Court Settlement on mutually agreed grounds.** This may be required in times of Strikes, Group Clashes and other issues of serious nature.

Mediation...

Mediation is also a Third party solution but a legal expert is not required in this procedure. A neutral person who has the expertise of dealing with such situations can be hired and consulted.

Problem Solving thus needs a set of abilities and competencies in the Head of the Institution. The Principal must allow his brain to serve him. If a problem is perceived and visualised on time, the solution becomes easier. **Proactive Role of Principal is therefore, very essential.** If the problem is taken as a challenge, tackled tactfully and timely, can be overcomed. The fellow employees as well the students should be **trained in such a manner that they come forward with solutions not the problems.**

Principal, therefore, needs to create a robust, speedy, self-reliant, secured and time bond mechanism for Problem Solving. **Principal has to play a bridging role in resolving conflicts and solving problems.**

Sometimes Problem is simple and the solution is also simple. But only a wise person can find such solution.

' A rich man died leaving his vast estate behind. Both sons quarreled over division. A wise man gave a simple solution. He suggested the elder one to divide the property in two equal parts on the bases of his sense of fairness and the second will have the First pick.'

What·an easy and apt solution.

CHAPTER XVII

Total Quality Management

Quality is defined as a continuous improvement in the product and service that we produce. It is a characteristic of our goods, things, services, behavior, tools and techniques. It is being excellent, much better than others, standard and superior.In Academic and Professional Institutions we often talk about Quality Education, Quality Teaching Learning, Quality Support System and Quality Results. Quality is now a Global phenomenon, a Global Movement. It is the most significant component of HRD.

Quality Education can transform the minds and Quality Principals and Teachers can change the world. Quality in Education is possible only when the team is passionately and relentlessly involved in shaping and guiding the young minds. Their outstanding performance is the testimony of their valuable contributions.

Quality means having value and free from defects. It satisfies the customers and fulfills their expectations and aspirations.

Quality concept first emerged in Industry and gradually procolated to almost all fields. Education is now the largest Global Industry striving for Quality and Excellence. It is not only the Quality Product but the process and service as well. In **brief the following are the features of Quality..**

It satisfies the customers and delights them.

Reliability and Durability.

Continual Improvement.

Consistent Excellence.

Standard and Reputation.

Fitness for the purpose of users.

Meeting the Competition.

Phenomenal Results

Quality Management is to direct and control the Organization with regard to Quality.

TotalQuality Management concept can be explained as under..

TOTAL..

Involving all functionaries to contribute their cent percent with excellence in their respected domains. It also encompasses all stakeholders, Environment and the Society.

QUALITY..

Being good, superior up to the expectations of customers. In Education, students, parents, and the community are the customers expecting quality education, quality teaching and quality results.

Management..

It is the process which makes all above happen ie the Leadership which initiates all efforts to achieve Quality.It is managing the men, money, material and machine to produce Quality Products.

Total Quality Management is therefore, a holistic and comprehensive approach to put the organization in right perspectives where the quality is the main focus and concern. TQM aims at accomplishing the goals for customer satisfaction.

Quality Approach is about...

Leadership by the top management. It provides vision, direction and resources for quality achievements.

1. **Customers Focused..**

Quality Management is primarily for fulfilling the expectations of customers by producing quality products. Quality Product for Educational Institutions is the student and result.

2. Involves all and develops Human Potentials.

Quality approach is inclusive. Both internal and external customers are prepared to serve the quality ie the employees and the students/parents. Only Quality employees can yield quality results.

3. Least wastage and defects..

While producing quality products and services, it is ascertained that no resource is wasted and every defect is prevented.

4. Trust, cooperative and coordinated approach..

TQM culture is built by mutual trust and cooperation. It lays the foundation of the success of TQM.

5. Improvement is Continuous Process in the TQM Approach.

Quality is directly related to improvement. TQM aims at improvement at every stage and every time.

6. Consistent Work Culture..

A cordial environment is necessary for TQM approach. In absence of a suitable work culture, quality can not be achieved.

Quality Related concepts..

Quality doesn't signify only TQM but there are several related terms..

Quality Control..

Quality can be achieved only when the control mechanism is strong. It is not only to exercise control but also to fulfill Quality Requirements.

Quality Assurance..

This to ascertain that all quality resources will be made available. It instills confidence in producers and customers about the quality.

Quality Improvement..

As stated earlier, quality refers to continuous improvement in the product as well as services.

Quality Policy..

Unless the Quality Policy by the Organization or the top Management is formulated, quality can not be achieved.

Quality Product is resultant to Quality Process and Quality Service.

Total Quality Management in Education.

Quality is not a new concept in Education. Right from the ancient time till today quality has been the prime concern. ***The Vedic Era, Gurukul System, various Education Policies, the Govts. All other Educational Organizations focused on Providing Quality Education.*** Therefore, the application of Total Quality Management in Education will bring drastic changes in Educational policies, processes and procedures.

Quality Education is a broad term. It is the end product of TQM. Unfortunately quality education is still a far cry in our country. Despite several policies, robust infrastructure, support system, amenities and huge expenditures, quality in education is yet not up to the expectations of the Stakeholders. The main reason behind this underachievement is ineffective implementation of TQM approach in Education. TQM in Education needs to be applied right from the formative stage.

Most often it has been noticed that the focus is on the Quality in Higher and Professional Education. The Primary and Secondary Education are still confined to policies. Therefore, there is an emergent need to overhaul the bottom line education system.

TQM is a managerial function. In Education it should be given a form of a movement which will bring several reforms for Quality Achievements. TQM approach can be applied in Education as follows.

Quality Planning..

Planning is the first and foremost process for the development and growth of every sector. We may not succeed in achieving the objective of Quality Education because of unsystematic or unthoughtful planning. Sometimes planning may be good but its ineffective implementation also adversely affects the growth. Therefore, a meticulous plan consisting of all quality concerns is essential. **The targets fixed should be realistic, achievable and measurable.**

TQM focuses on Designing the desired and deliverable quality standards, quality objectives and targets along with the Knowledge and set of skills required. The planning also deals with the Responsibility and Authority for effective implementation.

Quality Resource Management..

Whatever has been planned to provide Quality Education, Physical, Human and Financial Resources are required. Proper organization and management of these resources is necessary for effective implementation of proposed planning. Any wastage, underutilization and misuse of any of the resources will prove to be fatal for quality achievement.

TQM approach is Quality Centric not Cost centric. Quality improvement is certainly a Team Exercise. All Physical and Human Resources are managed in such a way that Quality becomes the first and foremost.

The Japanese Philosophy of KAIZEN is worth mentioning here. It is the main pillar behind the success of Japanese Industry. Kaizen is an inseparable aspect of Japanese TQM. It means continuous on going improvement or doing better than before. They firmly believe that all levels of people including the lowest one can contribute significantly to quality.

Quality Professionals..

It is the quality of the people which produces quality results. Quality Education is impossible without Quality Principals and Teachers. The Recruitment Process should focus on selecting the people who are well qualified, professionally trained, having love for the profession, academic bent of mind, aptitude and attitude. In fact we have not been able to provide Quality Education because of the nonavailability of Quality Principals and Quality Teachers. TQM is the answer to all this.

The following are the important traits of Quality Professionals..

Analytical and Innovative mind.

Commitment for Quality..

Capable and Confident..

Ability to work in teams.

Problem solving and decision making skills.

Effective communicator and motivator..

Positive to self and others.

Innovative Teaching Learning Strategies..

Even after creating 'A' class infrastructure and having qualified, trained and experienced faculty the purpose of quality education will be beyond reach if the Teaching Learning Practices are obsolete and outdated. It is only the Quality Instructional and Participative Process that leads to Quality Achievements. The teachers are required to enhance their teaching effectiveness by updating themselves in subject knowledge and teaching skills. Professional Development Courses organized from time to time are very useful.

Quality Learning Environment..

Building a cordial and congenial environment is perhaps the biggest Managerial Challenge. TQM practices lay much emphasis on creating a suitable work culture where the people *Earn as well as Learn.* In Academic and Professional Institutions, Learning is the foremost objective. The Learners won't be able to learn in absence of Proper Learning Environment. Indiscipline, disturbances, disruptions, non-cooperation, misunderstandings and poor status of interpersonal relationships spoil the overall functioning and cause hindrances in the Building of Learning Environment.

All employees want to learn provided they get opportunities and an environment to learn. *TQM approach aims at challenging the challenges.* Whatever obstacles arise in Environment Building can be removed if there is a will, conviction and commitment.

Capacity and Capability Building..

The capacity and capability have direct connection with quality. In an organization where the people are capable and able to contribute to their fullest capacity, quality is inevitable. TQM approach accords top priority to this aspect. In Educational Institutions several Professional Development Programs are organized for capacity and capability building including **On the Job and Off the Job training, workshops, symposiums, motivational techniques, incentives, rewards etc.**

Quality Leadership.

In an Institution all above are Leadership functions. An effective and efficient leader can only apply TQM tools and techniques for continuous improvement. **The leader must have the following Core Values for the application of TQM...**

- **Proactive Approach.**

- Excellence.
- Team Work
- Integrity.
- Self Confidence.
- Passion for Quality.
- Honesty and Transparency.
- Focus on Behaviour not on Person.
- Providing consistent Vision.
- System Thinking.

Principal should be able to turn the expenditure on Institutional Development into Investment. It can happen only when Quality is the focus. An unprecedented transformation can be brought through TQM. If applied systematically, The Institution can become most trusted and known for special features, innovations, results and Alumni placements. By **showcasing the Managerial** and **Leadership skills, the Principal will be able to reap all advantages of TQM.**

CHAPTER XVIII

Time Management

*"*Men talk of killing time, while time quietly kills them."*
-Dion Bouccecault."

Time is one of the most useful and Unique Resources. But different people use time differently. Some use time properly, some misuse it. Some are busy with business whereas some are busy without business. Some pass time, some waste time, some kill time. In Educational Institutions where the future of the nation is prepared and shaped, time is of greater importance. Principals are offly busy persons because of their academic, administrative and managerial duties. Teachers are too busy with their transactional work, corrections, evaluation, extra classes, non-academic duties and many others. Students are busy with their class and home assignments, revision, tests, exams etc. So there is hardly any spare time.

In DAY today's affairs time is to be managed in such a way that the assigned duties and responsibilities are performed efficiently in order to accomplish the task and achieve objectives. Time is always short, limited, whereas the works are unlimited and unending. Therefore, Effective Time Management is the Key Factor in the success of every Principal,Teacher and Student.

Time Management is one of the most important attributes of Leadership. It is a skill, an ability or technique to perform and achieve. The following are the unique features of time...
There is always scarcity of Time
The availability is the same to all i.e. 24 hrs.
Time gone never comes back.
Time can neither be switched on nor can be switched off.
It can neither be hired nor leased out.

Therefore
It can be managed only.

"Never leave till tomorrow which you can do today -
                            -Benjamin Franklin.
    "

Time does not heal anything, it just teaches us how to live with paucity of it. Time is money. Whosoever has understood, has learnt the Mantra of Success.

*Time*Wasters...

There are several time wasters which obstruct Effective Time Management. These can be summarised as under...

1.Personal...

Lack of Self-discipline..

Having no control over self, losing temper frequently, shouting, and snubbing waste lots of time. The time to be used in productive works is wasted due all this.

Indecisiveness...

When a person is not able to take even simple decisions, keeps the work pending and is suspicious, wastes much time.

Insecurity...

Feeling insecure in personal and professional affairs also causes wastage of time. It can be physical, mental or emotional. Sense of insecurity occupies the Principal elsewhere and the time for routine work is reduced.

Procrastination...

Doing yesterday's work today or postponing for the future. We waste much of our precious time this way.

Over cautious Approach.

Many people have an over cautious approach. They have several apprehensions. They get engaged in the status of confusion about doing the work or not.

Involving everyone.

Time is also wasted by unnecessarily involving more people than required to undertake a task.

Laziness..

Sometimes work is not done out of laziness. Laziness is a bad habit and therefore, becomes time waster.

2.Managerial...

a. Too much paperwork.

Paper work is essential in official procedures. **But excess of everything is bad.** The time of some constructive work is wasted in unnecessary paperwork. Paper work may not be required every time.

b. Multitasking.

Assigning and undertaking so many tasks at a time doesn't serve the purpose. May be task is not clear or not understood, work will be delayed resulting in time waste.

c. Unnecessary Meetings.

Meetings are necessary for smooth functioning but can also be avoided in many cases. It is often noticed that some meetings are conducted without the need and purpose.

3. Organisational.

a .Over and under staffing..

Both surplus and shortage of workforce may cause time waste. Over staffing spoils the work culture, leads to gossiping, conspiracies and other problems. Understaffing overburdens the employees causing stress and anxieties. In both situations work suffers and time is misused.

b. Uncongenial Work Environment..

Unfavourable working conditions and non--conducive environment of the organisation become time wasters as much time of the Head is spent in resolving the conflicts and solving problems of staff and students.

unsuitable

c. Non- supportive Head.

The most important function of the Principal is not only to direct and instruct but also to guide and motivate. Sometimes the

Principal may not be of supportive nature, the employees get demotivated and the work is not completed in stipulated time.

Time Management Techniques.

A. Three Ps of Time Management.

1.Planning

Plan your schedule for Effective Time Management.Even routine works should also be planned properly. The Principal must have a Planner mentioning what to do, when to do and how much time to be taken. Plan and potential are the essentials of Time Management.

2.Prioritizing.

Most people plan their work according to the pressure they feel rather than the priorities they have. **One has to be Proactive instead of Reactivte**. The Principal must list down his priorities and act accordingly. The rule of **First Things First needs to be** followed. The urgency of work must be known so that time is not wasted in undertaking the tasks which are not of urgent nature.

3. Performing.

After having planned and prioritised a task, it should be completed fully then only proceed further. It will enhance the Performance.The objective of the Head is to perform and monitor the Performance of others. We can perform better only when we have quality time at our disposal.

B. Develop self Discipline and Good Habits.

People who are not disciplined and don't cultivate good habits often waste time. They can never discipline others. For perfect Time Management one must be a disciplined person, develop good habits and positive lifestyle

C. Delegation..

Delegation is the ability to recognize the special potentials and limitations of team members. If you centralise the tasks to yourself, too much time will be taken and results won't be encouraging. Therefore, delegation of Authority as well the Responsibility is one of the best Time Management Techniques. .

D. Learn to work in blocks of time..

These days phone calls waste a lot of time. Principal needs to work in blocks of time , i.e. your phone, is for your convenience and not vice versa. Don't become slave of phone calls. Fix time to respond to calls. Be busy with business, Don't appear to be busy.

A person came to the office of the Principal. The Principal purposely lifted the receiver and kept talking. The person was surprised by the conversation. The Principal stopped for a while and asked the visitor to wait for some more time as he is discussing an urgent matter. After a few minutes the Principal kept the receiver. " Yes please, what can I do for you?" 'Nothing sir, I have come from the telephone exchange to connect your phone as it has been out of order for the last two days," replied the person.

E. Avoid Multitasking..

Getting involved in several works at a time and assigning in the same manner to others must be avoided. It is not only a time waster but also adversely affects productivity.

F. Settings Goals and Deadlines..

A good time manager has the ability to set the goals and deadlines to accomplish them. The goals can be personal as well as professional. These can be long term as well as short term. If this is not done, time is wasted in deciding the priorities.

Effective Time Management assists you to run your day failing which you run throughout the day. Life and time are the world's best teachers. Life teaches us to make the best use of time while time teaches us the value of life. Both are precious.

About The Author

R.P Dobhal

R.P Dobhal is a post graduate in English, Economics and M.Ed. He has the experience of about 40 years of teaching, educational administration and training. He has headed the training institutes of Navodaya Vidyalaya Samiti at Chandigarh and Ghaziabad. Besides, he has been Assistant Commisioner in Navodaya Vidyalaya Samiti Chandigarh. He is known for his academic acumenship, teachers training, educational planning and administration. After his retirement he has also served Sri Guru Ram Rai Education Mission Dehradun, one of the largest education body in North India as an Education Officer.

Shri RP Dobhal has the distinction of being an effective teacher trainer, academician and administrator. He has been sharing his vast and varied experiences in India as well as abroad. He is still into the field of training and conducts several training programs for educational administrators and teachers. Apart from dealing with several areas of teacher training, he is an expert of dealing with effective teaching-learning strategies. During his tenure as head of exclusively residential schools, he always experimented the tools and techniques to update the skills of the staff.

Connect With The Author

Youtube : RPD ACADEMICS

www.youtube.com/c/rpdacademics

RPD Academics is an educational channel that aims to promote effective teaching. Teaching is done, but effective teaching is rare. RPD Academics aims to increase the number of effective teachers. Videos that provide effective teaching strategies are frequently uploaded here. Please subscribe to the channel to get the latest videos about effective teaching.

• • •

FaceBook : rajendraprasad.dobhal

www.facebook.com/rajendraprasad.dobhal

• • •

Email : rpdobhal@gmail.com